Catherine Reynolds King

Cargo of Memories

**Saga of the *Majestic* Showboat – Last of the
Original and Authentic Floating Theatres
Still Operating in America**

Illustrated from rare photographs

**By
Catherine Reynolds King**

Cargo of Memories
First Edition

Dedication

In loving tribute to my father,
Captain Thomas Jefferson Reynolds

Captain Thomas Jeffeson Reynolds. Courtesy of *The Columbus Dispatch*.

Acknowledgements

I would like to thank my husband, Harry for his patience and encouragement during my years of writing and researching this book. Also my thanks to my daughter, Margaret Catherine Hudson, for her help in editing it.

Contents

Chapter 1
A Humble Beginning

Early in the spring of 1888 Francis Marion Reynolds brought his pregnant half-Shawnee Indian wife, Catherine Harmon, and their three-year-old daughter, Ida Mae, down the Ohio River from St. Marys to Point Pleasant, West Virginia.

They found housing in a log cabin overlooking the Ohio River near the point where the Great Kanawha River empties into the Ohio. The cabin was part of old Fort Randolph where a fierce battle had been fought between the Shawnee Indian Chief Cornstalk and Virginia Colonial Troops on October 10, 1774. My father, Thomas Jefferson Reynolds, was born in the cabin April 6, 1888.

Another son, William Henry, was born on April 2, 1892. By that time the family was living on a houseboat, one of several moored along the banks of the Ohio and Kanawha Rivers. A houseboat was a cheap and pleasant way for a family to live.

They managed on the few dollars earned working in construction during the summer and decked on steamboats in the winter.

Then a severe depression hit the country throwing everybody out of work. Catherine was confined to her bed with a terminal illness and they were destitute. There was no money to buy food or medicine and no one they could turn to for help.

Dad later told me "The clothes we kids wore were outgrown and hanging in shreds. We had to put layers of paper in our shoes to cover the holes. We nearly froze in the ice and snow. I knew what it was like to go to bed hungry every night. If it hadn't been for the catfish Pa caught, and the bread Franklin, a former negro slave, and Mrs. Gunn gave us, we probably would've starved. It was a time in our lives I'll never forget or let happen again if I can help it."

Dad was a typical Huckleberry Finn with his red hair, face splattered with freckles, and wide grin. His early childhood was spent playing with his brother Bill, Jake Heib, Ross Filson, Neil Gunn, Homer Smith, and other boys from the town. They played by the river, swimming, fishing, and floating on log rafts to faraway imaginary places.

They watched many boats go by, but they thought the beautiful white double-decked showboats were the most exciting of all. *French's Sensation, Robinson's Floating Opera,* and the *Water Queen* pulled into the landing with calliope playing and actors ballyhooing the show uptown with marching bands.

Though he had never seen a showboat performance, Dad was fascinated by the idea. "I'm gonna have a showboat like that when I grow up," he told the boys.

"Aw, Tommy, you're so poor you don't even have enough to eat, let alone thinking of buying a showboat," Jake said.

"I will! I will too!" he retorted with clinched fists. "You just wait and see, I'll show you all."

Dropping in at the Last Chance Saloon on Main Street was one of Dad's favorite pastimes. It was profitable, too. The men gave him nickles to dance the jig. He imitated the actors he'd seen perform on the street corner. No sooner had the money touched his palm than he went bouncing up and down like a jumping jack.

The men also gave him chewing tobacco and engaged in spitting contests with him. He made the old spittoon ping from across the room. One day, on a dare, he spit a mouthful of tobacco juice into the eyes of the sheriff's white mare tied up to the hitching post outside. When they finished laughing, the men gave him a quarter and he ran back to the houseboat and gave the quarter and the nickles he'd earned to his mother.

Shortly after his mother died, his father married Adah Hartman, and he put his boyhood days behind him. Thinking he could support himself, he dropped out of school at the age of nine and went to work helping fish for mussels.

From a slowly moving johnboat they drug a rod of brail lines across the mussel beds irritating the mussels into closing their shells over the pronged hooks. They brought in sizable catches every day. Then they boiled the mussels out in large vats, making an awful smell, and piled the shells on the riverbank. The owner of a mussel barge came by and paid them $3.00 a ton for the unclassified shells, and extra for pearls found in some of the mussels.

The answer to their financial problem was at their doorstep in the bounty of the river. It yielded a bumper crop of shells with mother-of-pearl linings and pearls for the taking. Dad saved his share of the money, continued to fish for mussels in the summer and worked at the Kanawha docks in the winter.

It was a busy time with boats undergoing repairs and new ones being built as the economy improved. There was no child labor law then. Dad was paid twenty-five cents a day to pump water and serve as errand boy to the carpenters. It was there, as he advanced from one job to another, that he learned the boat carpenter trade.

While still in his teens he built a mussel barge and bought a 15 horsepower gas towboat named *Kate Paden* in partnership with his pa and brother. The barge had separate compartments for hauling mussel shells according to their classification and value.

Then, with the barge and family houseboat in tow of the *Kate Paden,* they traveled the Ohio and Muskingum Rivers fishing for mussels and buying shells and pearls from other fishermen. When they had a barge load they sold the shells for $12 to $15 a ton to a button factory in Portsmouth, Ohio, and the pearls, at an even larger profit, to a jeweler. Meanwhile, Dad learned to pilot the boat.

As they continued to prosper they added another barge and sidewheel ferryflat to their fleet. The barge was used to haul scrap iron, copper, rope, etc. they found lying along the riverbank, and sold to a junk dealer.

The ferryflat housed a team of work mules and a heavy duty wagon they used to haul their cargo. They combed the countryside buying junk from the farmers to resell at a profit.

Moses McGlone and his teenaged son Steven were hired to help with the work. Moses, who lived at Portsmouth, Ohio, had two lovely young daughters who came down to the boat to visit while they worked. Margaret (Maggie), a demure redhead, caught Dad's fancy. Fannie, a vivacious blond, soon had Bill thinking that she was the only girl in the world for him.

Dad's big break came when he was 21 years old, with a little help from big sister Ida. Following a bad marriage at thirteen, Ida had struck out on her own. She returned fashionably dressed in silk and furs, wearing a two and a half carat diamond engagement ring. Her fiance, Thomas "Tegie" Nicol, was an accomplished musician and gentleman racehorse enthusiast from Chicago. He owned several race horses and loved to gamble. His brother Dave was a professional jockey.

Tegie admired Dad for his determination to get ahead and wanted to go into a new business venture with him.

"What kind of business?" Dad asked.

"A dish and tinware tradeboat," Tegie replied. "We can sell everything from fine eggshell china and cut glass crystal to graniteware. I bet we could really clean up."

So, sealing their partnership with a handshake, they started marking plans.

Dad married Maggie McGlone in a double wedding ceremony with sister Ida and Tegie Nicol. Bill married Maggie's younger sister Fannie.

They built their tradeboat in the fall and winter of 1909-1910 at Point Pleasant and named her the *Illinois* The boat was twenty feet wide and a hundred feet in length. It looked like a showboat when it was finished. The first deck housed the dish and tinware shop and the second deck was living quarters for the owners. It consisted of two 3-room apartments divided by a breezeway and stairs leading into the showroom.

They also bought a secondhand gas towboat named the *Liberty*, for $15, to transport the *Illinois* and ferryflat.

The storeroom was stocked with Imperial Glass and graniteware from Bellaire; china and pottery from Zanesville and East Liverpool, Ohio; and tin and ironware from Pittsburgh.

They made two or three day stopovers at small towns along the Ohio and Muskingum Rivers. Mother, Ida, and Tegie waited on customers who came down to the boat. Dad drove the vendor's wagon through the countryside selling wares to the farm wives.

If they didn't have cash he traded for like value in farm produce. He'd trade a cup and saucer for milk, a matching plate for butter, water glass for eggs, a pitcher for a stewing hen, an iron skillet for a slab of smoked bacon, or bean pot for a bushel of green beans. That way he never missed a sale and he kept the table supplied with all the food they could eat. He made extra money selling the surplus in the boat store.

Dad liked quail eggs. One day while Mother was gathering firewood from along the shore, she found a nest. When she broke one of the eggs into the skillet, out popped a baby snake writhing in the sizzling grease. The family never let her live it down.

Though mother was used to having all the modern conveniences of a city dweller, she took to the way of life on the river. It was a good life, but a hard one for a woman. In addition to her shop and housework duties she did everything from carrying water, chopping wood, swabbing the decks and pulling lines, to learning to pilot the boat. It was a rarity then for women to be given a chance to pilot a boat.

The only time she took a break was when she gave birth to sons, Marion and Norman, and daughter, Hazel, aboard the *Illinois*.

One day, in the summer of 1912, they stopped where a small moving-picture showboat was playing. Though silent pictures were being shown in large cities, movie boats were the first to introduce film to the small river towns.

The operator, who was short of help, asked Dad to take up tickets for the show that evening. The more he watched people filing into the theater the more excited he became about the possibility of showing moving pictures aboard the *Illinois*. At ten cents each it was the easiest money he'd ever seen made.

The owner was willing to sell, so he took the movie equipment aboard the *Illinois*. They made it a moving-picture showboat which they successfully operated along with their dish and tinware business.

The theater was lighted with oil lamps and had bench seats for two hundred people. The entrance and ticket office was through the dish shop. That way men bought fancy dishes for their ladies after the show.

Dad hand cranked the movie projector. Tegie provided mood music on the piano. Mother and Ida sold and took up tickets. They presented world news briefs, cartoon strips and silent movies of Charlie Chapman, Fattie Arbuckle, Douglas Fairbanks and Mary Pickford, and many more.

Song slides encouraged the audience to join in the finale, singing "In the Shade of the Old Apple Tree," "By the Light of the Silvery Moon," and "Let Me Call You Sweetheart." Meanwhile, Uncle Bill and Grandpa turned the family houseboat into a fifty seat moving picture boat they named the *Pastime Theatre*. Though tiny, their showboat brought the world to movie starved inhabitants along the river. With Grandpa or Uncle Bill at the helm, they stopped at villages that had been passed by the larger showboats.

The *Illinois* remained open the year-round for business, weather permitting. Seven months were spent in transit on the river and five in winter harbor, but the career of the *Illinois* was short lived.

August 5, 1916, they stopped at Foster, Kentucky for a three day engagement. The day began as usual. Dad hitched the team to the vendor's wagon. With a great clattering of pots and pans he drove the wagon off the ferryflat and headed out through the countryside peddling his wares. Marion and Norman rang the bell on the head of the wagon to attract attention as they approached farm houses. By the time they pulled to a stop the entire family had gathered outside to see the merchandise.

After making a sale for cash or trade, he told them about the moving picture show aboard the *Illinois* that evening and moved on to the next stop.

Working their way back to Shultz Landing they stopped to visit Grandpa, Uncle Bill, and Aunt Fan, who now had three children, Bill Jr., Ida Mae, and Raymond. Their boat, the *Pastime Theatre,* was showing 3.2 miles downriver from Foster.

Dad and the boys returned to the *Illinois* with a pocketful of money, all the fresh fruit, vegetables, and meat they could use.

Hopping in the skiff they rowed across the river to a sandbar where they picked up fuel coal that had fallen off barges making the sharp turn at the head of the bar. Wading waist deep in the water, Dad located pieces of coal with his foot and the boys dove after them. By supper time they had a nice load of coal and returned to the boat.

As customary, Mother had left fourteen month old Hazel asleep in her crib while she sold tickets. Marion and Norman had raced to the front of the theatre where they sat every night watching the moving pictures.

A capacity crowd had gathered on board. Dad showed the news reel, a comedy film, and had started the main feature, *"The Great Train Robbery."*

Suddenly, a red light flashed across the screen blotting out the film characters. A spark from the projector had caught the highly flammable film on fire, igniting the extra reels of film on a nearby storage shelf, and setting the walls on fire. There was no stopping it.

In seconds the booth was a blazing inferno.

"Fire! Fire! The boat's on fire!" the frantic cry rose from the crowd and they began running and screaming from the theatre.

"Women and children first!" Uncle Tegie yelled as he left the piano to direct them off the boat.

Panicked men, women, and children jammed the narrow passageway through the dish shop as flames licked toward them. They were slowed again on deck by the narrow gangplank leading off the boat.

Mother caught a glimpse of Marion and Norman running from the theatre with some other boys. She ran upstairs and got Hazel out of bed, grabbed the money she and Dad had saved, and tucked it under Hazel's clothing. Then she dashed back downstairs and handed Hazel to a woman who was leaving the theatre with her children.

"Don't worry Mrs. Reynolds, I'll look after her," the lady assured her.

Mother quickly joined some men from the crowd who had a bucket brigade going. One of the theatre windows was knocked out. They drew water from the river and passed it through to the workers inside.

The boat was made of highly combustible rosin lumber. It bled and burst into flames from the scorching heat like setting a torch to gasoline. The fire quickly spread into the theatre, upper deck, and dish shop.

What had been a wonderful place of fun and laughter had become a smoke filled chamber of terror to the people waiting to get out. Some of them panicked and leaped through the windows, off the front deck into the river, and swam ashore to escape the fire. They all made it to safety.

The team of mules on the ferryflat, moored alongside the *Illinois*, leaped the railing into the river to get away from the scorching heat. Afraid the tanks of gas he had stored aboard the *Liberty* would explode, Dad cut the lines with a fire ax, setting her adrift on the river. Then he went back to fighting the fire, staging one last desperate attempt to save the showboat.

The fire continued to rage out of control. Finally, with the family the last to leave, they had to give up. Dad dove into the river and swam after the *Liberty*. The wind and current had banked her three quarters of a mile downstream on the opposite side of the river.

Then Grandpa arrived on the scene. He had been showing to a full house of moviegoers aboard the *Pastime Theatre* when he saw a red glow in the sky. At first he thought it was from the side-wheel excursion, *Island Queen,* that had passed by earlier. But, as the sky continued to grow brighter, he realized that Dad was in trouble. Cranking up the engine aboard the *Kate Paden,* he had left the showboat behind and come as fast as he could. Seeing that the fire was beyond control, he went down inside the smoke filled hull and knocked a hole in the gunnel with a sledgehammer. That allowed the boat to sink and burn itself out.

Meanwhile, Mother discovered that Norman was missing. He wasn't in the large crowd of people on the riverbank watching the fire. Marion was there with his friends from the town, but not Norman!

"Where's your brother?" she asked.

"I don't know" Marion answered, watching the fire.

"When was the last time you saw him?" she asked.

"When we was watching the moving pictures. I was asleep when the people woke me up screaming. They were running, so I got up and went with them," he said.

"Oh, my God!" Mother screamed. "Norman's still on the boat! In the fire! My poor baby!" She ran back to the boat to look for him.

It was all Ida and Tegie could do to stop her. "Stay here, Maggie, I'll go," Uncle Tegie gently told her.

He tied a wet handkerchief around his nose and mouth, and disappeared inside the doomed showboat. He worked his way through the fire, water, and fallen timbers, to the front of the theatre where he last saw Norman. There he found the boy lying on the burning seat with his hair and clothing on fire. Smothering the flames with his bare hands, Tegie, with Norman in his arms, ran out the stage door, leaped into the river and swam ashore.

Norman was still alive, but severely burned. He died shortly afterwards.

The little redheaded boy mother had seen running from the theatre with Marion was a boy from the town. He looked like Norman.

Dad later told me, "I was a good piece downriver when I stopped swimming and treaded water long enough to look back at the fire. The *Illinois* was engulfed in flames, lighting up the sky. It was heartbreaking watching her go up in smoke. Then I heard someone screaming. It sounded like your mother, but I was too far away to turn back, so I got the *Liberty* and returned as soon as I could. Tegie was waiting to tell me the horrible news. God, it was awful! I fell to my knees and cried like a baby at the sight of Norman's charred body lying on the ground."

With all the family and townspeople present, graveside rites were held for Norman the following day in the rain. A local resident very kindly let them bury Norman in his pioneer family cemetery near the boat landing. Dad placed a wooden marker he carved out of oak driftwood at the gravesite. It read: Norman Reynolds - son of Thomas J. and Margaret Reynolds - Born 1912 - Died 1916.

Back at the boat landing the family sadly gazed at the empty place where the *Illinois* had stood the day before.

The fire had burned throughout the night and the boat's superstructure, furnishings and equipment were all destroyed. Thanks to Grandpa's quick thinking, the hull was saved. It was given to him and Uncle Bill for salvage.

Making the *Liberty* their temporary home, they moved on to rebuild and take up their lives without Norman.

The money Mother and Aunt Ida had saved from their quarters aboard the burning *Illinois* provided the ready cash to build the next showboat – the *America*.

The hull for the *America* was built at Vanceburg, Kentucky, and its superstructure at Huntington, W. Va. the winter of 1916-1917. The boat was twenty by a hundred feet in length, same as the *Illinois*.

Before all the windows and doors were installed, mother gave birth to another son. Thomas Jefferson, Jr. was born March 12, 1917.

The *America* was a drama and vaudeville showboat, the ultimate in river entertainment, with a professional troup of actors and musicians.

The theatre consisted of a stage with handpainted sets, the main floor and balcony, with the overall seating capacity for 300 people. Other features included electric lights, opera seats, ceiling fans, and steam radiated heat for cold weather. It had all the modern conveniences of the time except indoor plumbing.

Entrance to the theatre was in the center front deck with ticket window on the left. A wide stairway led off the front deck to the balcony.

Three of the actors' staterooms and the Nicols' two roomed apartment were on the upper front deck. Aunt Ida had a secret stairway leading from their living room into the ticket office. Dad's family had a similar apartment on the back upper deck of the showboat.

The backstage area doubled as kitchen and dining room for the family and actors. There were two extra staterooms aboard the *Liberty* towboat.

The *America* was painted red, white and blue. It had a 32 note whistle steam calliope installed on the roof deck. A boiler on the stern of the showboat provided steam to play the calliope and generated electricity.

My family built two showboats that winter and spring of 1916-1917. Grandpa and Uncle Bill gave Dad and Uncle Tegie a hand in getting the *America* under roof. Then they built another double decked boat on the salvaged hull of the *Illinois*. It became a 300 seat moving picture and vaudeville showboat called the *Superior Theatre* and replaced the small *Pastime Theatre*.

The *America* opened her first season at Point Pleasant, W. Va. early in April 1917. They presented the four act drama "*Bertha, the Sewing Machine Girl*," and four vaudeville acts sandwiched in between acts of the play.

When the first draft of World War 1 became effective, Dad and Uncle Tegie both registered, but they were never called to active duty.

The *America* traveled along the river with Old Glory waving in the breeze and Uncle Tegie at the calliope keyboard playing patriotic songs. The *America* soon gained recognition as the finest amusement craft afloat for its size.

They traveled the Ohio, Monongahela, and great Kanawha rivers, where the steel mills and chemical plants worked around the clock producing war materials.

All the towns were enjoying a hefty upswing in economy, so the showboat cashed in on it, too. They stayed out with the *America* until it became too cold to operate. Then they tied up at Henderson, West Virginia, opposite Point Pleasant, for the winter.

I arrived on the scene December 19, 1918. The family was in winter harbor following their second tour with the *America*. Winter had set in early, dumping tons of snow in the valley, and the rivers had frozen over. Then there was a warming trend, followed by heavy rains. That triggered an ice run, one of Mother Nature's most violent and destructive forces. The Kanawha River was running brimful of ice packs past the showboat into the ice filled Ohio River. Suddenly an ice pack hit the showboat. The lines snapped and the *America* and *Liberty* were torn loose from the landing. They were carried out of the mouth of the Kanawha onto the broad Ohio in the ice run.

At this very time I made my dramatic entrance into this world. Doctor Barbee couldn't make it to the boat for obvious reasons. Aunt Ida helped mother deliver me, while Dad and Uncle Tegie frantically worked below deck to save the boats. Finally, with other boatmen rushing to our aid, the *America* and *Liberty* were brought to a safe landing two miles downriver from Henderson.

Dad reportedly took one look at me, a carbon copy of the other kids with my red hair and blue eyes, and named me Catherine after his mother.

I was healthy and strong until my third birthday. Then I was stricken by infantile paralysis which resulted in the impairment of my left leg and right foot. We were in winter quarters at Pittsburgh during an epidemic of the disease in that area. The doctors and child specialists could offer no hope that I'd ever be able to walk again.

For six highly successful seasons my family toured the rivers with the *America*, presenting famous old plays: "*From Rags to Riches, Kentucky Sue, Tess of the Storm Country, Abie's Irish Rose,*" etc., plus vaudeville specialties.

They charged $1.00 admission for adults and 50 cents for children under twelve, and played to sold-out houses. Some of the people even paid their dollar to stand on the front deck and watch the show through the double doors of the theatre. In some places they had to turn people away every night due to lack of space in the auditorium. A larger showboat was obviously needed.

So, at the close of their 1922 season, Dad and Uncle Tegie pooled their money once again and built another larger showboat, the *Majestic.*

Chapter 2
I Watched the Building
of the *Majestic*

Construction of the Majestic got underway in November 1922 at Clyde's Landing, Glenwood, Pennsylvania, on the Monongahela River near Pittsburgh.

Shortly after the *America* and *Superior* Showboats had harbored for the winter, a shipment of lumber arrived from Oregon. The B&O Railway made a side stop to unload the lumber at the construction site. Rosin lumber was used again for its durability and resistance to dry rot. It also came in extra long timber lengths for a minimum of splicing.

Dad was carpenter and designer and Uncle Tegie was his assistant. Grandpa, Uncle Bill, Mother, and Aunt Ida were their helpers. Mother divided her time between doing housework, looking after the children, carrying lumber, and manning one end of the crosscut saw. Marion and Hazel also had special jobs to do after attending classes at public school. Young Tommy served as errand boy to the workers.

Although I was only four years old that winter, I have vivid recollections of sitting by our living room and kitchen windows aboard the *America* watching as they built the new showboat.

They took great pride in doing all the work themselves. Dad was the first one on the job at the crack of dawn and the last to lay down his tools at night.

First they made a wide clearing on the riverbank sloping down to the river where there was a three-foot dropoff. Then they set up two parallel rows of stocks where the framework for the *Majestic's* flat bottomed hull was laid out. It measured 26 by 120 feet, by 4 feet deep. They soon had the hull built.

Next, they cut and trimmed poles from trees along the river bank and used them to build the launching ramp, made slippery with axle grease. A towline was run from the *Liberty* to the barge. In split second timing the stocks were knocked out from underneath the front side of the hull. Dad backed the *Liberty* out into the river, pulling the bow and then the stern of the hull onto the launching ramp. With every available person pushing from behind, away it went, sliding sideways toward the river. Splashing into the water, it dipped down, listing heavily and bounced back up floating high and dry.

Then construction of the double-decked superstructure and pilothouse got underway. I could look down at the family as they hurried to and fro laying the main deck. It wasn't long until they were outside my window laying the floor to the second deck.

The boat rocked underfoot from the waves in the wake of passing steamboats. Then the river froze over and zero temperatures made construction difficult. Spring rains, ice run, and a flood didn't deter them from getting the job finished.

Hundreds of light bulbs, purchased bulk rate from a local factory outlet, were delivered to us by motorboat. They were packed loose in bushel baskets. Mother and I wiped them clean of factory dust before they were installed inside the theatre and along the entire length of the showboat and pilothouse, lighting the *Majestic* like a birthday cake.

An entrance with double French doors led into the theatre with ticket window on the left. A staircase led upstairs to the balcony and peanut heaven. There were also box seat compartments next to the stage.

Downstairs the main aisle led through two general admission sections. There were three reserved sections down front and more box seats adjoined the stage.

The stage was twelve feet high, twelve feet deep, and twenty feet wide. The orchestra pit had room to squeeze in six or seven skinny musicians. It was four feet wide by sixteen feet long and reached by a stairway under the stage. Seating capacity of the *Majestic* was 425 people. There were 300 seats on the main floor and 125 in the balcony and box seats, with room for expansion.

The theatre interior had white flower-embossed metal ceilings. There were ornamental light shades, pastel green walls with varnished trim, maroon seats and draperies. Black wooden trellises entwined with red rambling roses and green ivy adorned the sides of the stage. There were steam radiators for heat and open wall fans through which cool air could be drawn in off the river.

Dressing rooms were backstage. From there a bell could be rung as an emergency alarm, breakfast bell, or call to rehearsals.

Our apartment was on the upper back deck of the showboat. It consisted of a 16 x 16 foot living room bedroom combination. Mom and Dad slept there in a four poster brass bed. There was an adjoining 12 x 16 foot fully equipped kitchen for off tour use. Marion, Tommy, Hazel and I, slept in space saving double bunk beds built into the kitchen wall. They were curtained off from view during the day. A wall transom next to my lower bunk overlooked part of the wings and stage. I could lay there and watch the actors taking their cues and performing on stage each night.

Uncle Tegie and Aunt Ida took the apartment on the front deck of the showboat. They handled business affairs and tended the ticket office. Their apartment was built like ours. They also had a wide, glass panelled door opening onto the front deck where they and the crew could sit, relax, and enjoy the scenery. Aunt Ida had two dogs. She also had hundreds of canaries she raised and sold.

From the pilothouse on the *Majestic* Dad could see in all directions. It was more practical to navigate the boats from there instead of the towboat. The steering gear, with disconnectable cables running to the engine room aboard the towboat, consisted of the wheel, forward and reverse clutch, idle and stop clutch, and an air whistle for signalling maneuvers. The polished oak steering wheel and Dad's captain chair were the only purchased items. Dad made the clutches out of scrap lumber. The air whistle control, operated by his foot, was nothing more than the end of a broomstick.

His framed Pilot License, issued by the U. S. Army Corps of Engineers, Pittsburgh District, was displayed on the wall above the steering wheel. It granted him the right to navigate the *Majestic* on the Ohio River System from Pittsburgh, Pa. to Cairo, Illinois. It was a "long license" tempered with the fact that he was his own master and owner of the boat.

Finally, with the printing of the name *Majestic* in red and black shaded letters al;ong the sides of the showboat, and the Nicol and Reynolds insignia on the pilothouse, our bigger and better showboat was a reality.

Uncle Tegie named her *Majestic* after a popular theatre in Chicago. With her completion in March 1923, she joined thirteen other showboats gearing up for the spring season. They were the *America, Water Queen, Princess, Goldenrod, French's New Sensation, Bryant's Showboat, Valley, Columbia, River Maid, Sunny South, Rex, Cotton Blossom,* and the *Nineteenth Century.*

Now we had three showboats. One too many, since none of the Reynolds boys was old enough or experienced enough to run one of them. So, the *America* showboat and *Liberty* towboat were turned over to Grandpa and Uncle Bill to operate.

They sold the *Superior Theatre* to the Zubick Salvage Company at Pittsburgh for use as a houseboat, and junked the towboat *Superior,* formerly the *Kate Paden.*

A new towboat for the *Majestic* was required so they looked over the salvaged hull of a gas towboat, named *Atta Boy.* It had recently lost its double-decked superstructure in a fire. They wanted a gas towboat because it was more economical than steam and required only one licensed pilot. The hull was 22 x 75-feet long and had its 40hp Fairbanks Morse engine and paddle wheel still intact. The price was right, so they bought it, rebuilt it, and renamed it the *Atta Boy.*

The *Atta Boy's* main deck housed the engine room, the power-house for the *Majestic.* In addition to the twin-belted engine running nearly the full length of the boat, it had a brass steam dynamo to generate electricity for the theater, a generator for alternate house current, and a motorized water pump for fighting fires.

The *Atta Boy's* pilothouse was equipped with an oak steering wheel, clutches and an air whistle for use separate from the *Majestic.* There was also a stateroom and L-shaped dining room and kitchen, equipped with a round oak dining room table and chairs, cupboard, coal range; and large oversized cookware that hung on the wall.

The dining room held Tegie's pump organ for practicing calliope music, an oblong table with seating for twelve people, a drinking fountain, and an ice box. A door opened onto a utility deck with wash tubs and a community privy. All the comforts of home.

A calliope was installed on the roof deck of the *Atta Boy.* It was purchased from the Thomas Nicol Manufacturing Plant in Cincinnati for $450 and was the largest calliope made by this firm.

A brass console, the calliope had thirty two graduated whistles. When played on eighty pounds of steam pressure its music could be heard from three to five miles away depending on which the wind was blowing. Nothing could equal its magnificent "voice" in announcing our arrival at the landings.

A boiler at the stern of the showboat provided steam for the calliope, lights, radiators, and for heating bath water. All we had to do was hang a bucketful of river water on a pipe attached to the boiler, release steam into it, and presto, we had hot water. In places where we couldn't get fresh water, the boiler provided distilled water for drinking and cooking purposes. It had a terrible taste, but served its purpose.

The showboat, towboat combination was a self sustaining community and capable of going anywhere we wanted to take her for long periods of time. She wasn't too big to navigate the smaller less accessible rivers, or to make passage through miniature size locks and hairpin curves. Nor was she too heavy, with her 14-inch draft, to float over a mere trickle of water. She was also large enough to accommodate veteran crowds of showboaters along the Ohio and Mississippi River.

My family was unique because they built their own showboats and towboats at a minimum of cost. The *Majestic* alone would have cost over $20,000 had she been built at a commercial shipyard. The overall cost of building and outfitting our new showboat and towboat was $7,000. And it only took them six months of unceasing labor to accomplish it!

Organizing the Show

Uncle Tegie began organizing the show in February. The Robert J. Sherman Play Company in Chicago sent a number of manuscripts for his approval. *"Bloomer Girl,"* caught his attention. It became a smash hit on Broadway at the Shubert Theater in 1944. It was a story about women in their pursuit of freedom, trying to get out of hoopskirts, and their involvement in the underground railroad at the onset of the Civil War.

Two other plays, *"Fighting for Honor"* and *"Lena Rivers,"* were chosen and kept in reserve for alternate presentations. A royalty fee of $15 per play granted us the use of them during the tour. A similar fee was also paid to the American Society of Composers, Authors and Publishers for the copyrighted music used in the shows and for the calliope.

We could get all the actors we needed by running a classified ad in *Billboard* magazine, the actor's bible. Actors wouldn't be caught dead without the latest edition. It kept them well informed of job opportunities around the country.

There were many actors who would gladly accept our vacation package deal of $30 a week plus room and board. They only had three hours of work each day, Monday through Saturday. The rest of the time they could do as they pleased. Most of them were used to doing two or three shows a day and living out of their suitcases as they moved from town to town and theatre to theatre.

Not just any actor would do. The showboat actor was unique. They had to be adept in doubling dramatic parts, singing, dancing, and comedy. They also had to be sober and able to get along well with others. Compatibility was very important to keep the operation running smoothly. After all, they would be living, sleeping and working with us like one of the family aboard the boat for seven months.

Although Dad and Tegie were easygoing, Aunt Ida was not. She kept everybody in line, on their toes, and ran a tight ship. Actors could be easily replaced.

Our first ad for actors to tour with the *Majestic* appeared in the March 31, 1923 issue of the *Billboard*:

> "*Majestic Showboat* Wants Vaudeville people doing parts, or dramatic people with specialties, six shows a week. A few bills a season. No kids or pets. State lowest, if double piano advise. Boat owned and managed by former owners of the *America*. New in every detail. Open second week in April. Nicol and Reynolds, Hazelwood Station, Pittsburgh, Pa."

Letters with publicity photos and resumes came from both amateurs and veteran performers wanting to make the tour. There was the usual number of actors and would-be actors from the Pittsburgh area who came in person to the boat looking for a job. A number of mothers brought their children in costumes to audition for a spot in the show. Even circus performers applied. One man wanted to hire on as a high diver.

"I can make my dive off the top front deck of the showboat into the river as we're pulling into the landing. It would make a good publicity stunt for your new showboat," he told Uncle Tegie.

"Yes, it would," Uncle replied, "But it's too dangerous. There could be anything submerged, lying under the water. We can't take a chance on you breaking your neck."

Finally, three married teams and one single actor were hired. Married teams were preferred because Dad and Tegie thought they made less trouble than singles. They were wired money for tickets and the date to join the showboat.

They arrived on schedule with their bags and trunks at the Glenwood Train Station and walked the short distance up the dirt landing road to the boat. We could tell they were show people by the proud way they walked and by their flashy clothing. They looked like real city slickers.

The troupe included Samuel Lippencott, a distinguished middle aged actor, trombone player, and director of the show; his wife, Josephine, character actress and saxophonist; Claude Clark, leading man and coronetist; Mary Clark, leading lady and clarinetist. Frank "Rusty" Barton, comedian, trap drummer and scenic artist (formerly with the *America*). He had also appeared with the Spawn Family show out of Point Pleasant. Naomi Barton, ingenue and dancer; and Frank Cannon, parts, music director, piano and calliope player.

The Lippencotts, Clarks, and Bartons were shown to their staterooms on the upper deck of the showboat. Their furnished rooms were 8 x 10 feet long. Frank Cannon was given the stateroom on the lower front deck of the boat. The actors would receive a once a week linen service. Mother washed their linen, hung it out to dry, ironed and delivered it to their door.

A meal of stewed chicken and dumplings, mashed potatoes, gravy, green beans, peas, coleslaw, biscuits and apple pie was waiting for them on that first night aboard.

Dad, sitting at the head of the table, was served first. Then all formalities were dropped as everybody helped themselves to all the food they could eat. We four kids ate together around the kitchen table.

After the meal, Dad, Tegie and the actors remained seated at the table drinking coffee, smoking and getting acquainted. It was a scene that would be repeated countless times during my years of growing up aboard the showboat. Being confined to a chair because of my handicap, I was allowed to sit in the dining room while Mother, Ida, and Hazel were busy in the kitchen.

Everybody smoked. Dad puffed on a cigar, Tegie had a fancy clay pipe with a lion's head, while the actors and actresses smoked one hand-rolled cigarette after the other.

They kept up a constant flow of stories about the theatres, actors, and places they'd worked before joining the boat. Their speech and mannerisms were typical of people in the profession. An actor was always on stage and they seemed very sophisticated compared to the Reynolds family.

They all gathered for the reading rehearsal of *"Bloomer Girl."* Director Lippencott handed out parts and pencils. All suggestive words, actions, and profanity had to be replaced with more acceptable dialogue. The word "Damn," had to be marked out as it was offensive to some of the river audience at the time. The word "God," used out of context could cause the sheriff to stop the show, make us return the patron's hard earned money, and prevent us from stopping at his town again.

The showboat, as I personally knew it, was a place where a man could bring his whole family and spend an enjoyable evening out without fear of being embarrassed. A good, clean family type show was our motto and trusted trademark.

Daily rehearsals of the play were held until everyone knew their parts. Then, with special attention given to my sister Hazel's Irish song and dance debut, vaudeville and band rehearsals were held.

Meanwhile, Frank Barton and Uncle Tegie found time to design and build scenery. It had to be custom built to fit the stage. Each set consisted of six to eight sections of wood frames covered with muslin that Mother stitched on the sewing machine. As each set was finished they laced the sides together and gave them two coats of calcimine paint. Then Frank painted on the artwork.

The special costumes for the play, bloomers, hoop skirt dresses, fancy shawls and capes, ringlet wigs, picture hats, etc. were rented as part of a package deal from the play company. The costumes had to be altered to fit the players, so Mother became seamstress and wardrobe mistress for the cast.

The posters of the "Bloomer Girl" in her controversial costume, and the announcement of the new Nicol and Reynolds *Majestic Showboat* were also obtained from the same company.

Dad and thirteen-year-old Marion teamed up as advance men for the boat. They plastered the posters on the sides of business establishments and barns in the outlying areas until it looked like the Barnum and Bailey Circus coming to town.

The *Majestic* also had to undergo a Coast Guard inspection of her hull and boiler before we could get our Safety at Sea accreditation to go on tour. Without it we were not allowed to move the showboat away from the landing.

Frank Cannon fine-tuned the calliope and played a number of our favorite songs. How beautiful it sounded to us.

Just one week after the actors joined the boat and rehearsals got underway, we were ready to embark on our first tour with the *Majestic*.

Chapter 3
Here Comes the Showboat

April 9, 1923, Dad was the first one up aboard the showboat. He roused the boys out of bed and they followed him to the lower deck where they were joined by Uncle Tegie. Like Marion, Tommy was learning showboatin' from the deck up.

Going to the riverbank, the boys untied the lines. Dad and Tegie pulled the lines in and stacked them in neat piles on deck. The clicking of the manually operated capstan on the *Atta Boy* winding in wire cable, and the loud thump of the gangplank being pulled in and dropped into traveling position on the head of the boat, roused everybody else out of bed.

The actors and actresses in bathrobes and hair done up in rag curlers were gathered on deck outside their staterooms. Hazel, Aunt Ida, and Queenie, her poodle, were on the upper front of the boat watching. Mother, with me on her lap, sat on the back deck in a rocking chair.

Dad started the engine by lighting the gasoline fuse and turning the big flywheel with his foot. Then, when he reached the pilothouse, he sounded the departure whistle.

"All clear below deck! Move her out!" yelled Aunt Ida, who was voluntarily taking the place of first mate. She leaned out over the fence railing and relayed the signals up to him again to make sure he had heard it.

Another toot of the whistle immediately followed, signaling our intention to leave port and warned other boats to steer clear.

Skillfully, Dad nosed the showboat out into the middle of the river and we proceeded to Elrama, Pa., the first stop on our itinerary. It was nineteen nautical miles from Glenwood.

Making passage through our first locks with the *Majestic,* at Lock and Dam No. 2, was fascinating. Pulling up to the lock approach, one long and one short toot of our whistle sounded to make passage.

One long toot of the lock whistle granted permission. Then the attendant caught our line with a wire hook and walked along the top of the wall with us. We moved inside the deep, moss covered chamber and glided to a stop near the exit. The automatic gates closed behind us, the floodgates were opened and the chamber filled with surging water. Up we went, elevating an inch or so at a time to the upper pool maintained for safe navigation above the locks.

Meanwhile, the actors in their fancy knickers climbed up the lock ladder to the walkway on top where they had a better view. Marion and Tommy made trips to and from the lockhouse filling our buckets and drinking fountain with fresh water, courtesy of Uncle Sam. Dad signed the Lock Register. Then, when the boats finished elevating to the twelve-foot mark on the lock gauge, the lockage was completed. It took twenty minutes. The upper gates opened and the whistle sounded for our departure.

Dad stopped talking to the lock master and returned to the pilothouse, the actors scrambled back on board, and with a farewell toot of our whistle we chugged merrily out of the locks and resumed our trip.

The aroma of breakfast filled the air. We had bacon, eggs, french toast or hot biscuits, one morning and pancakes the next. There were no variations.

The actors made a beeline to the dining room. Mother took a man-sized tray of coffee and pancakes to Dad in the pilothouse. Uncle Tegie and Marion ate in shifts so one of them could always be on deck duty.

Mother kept the hot cakes coming off the griddle while Aunt Ida stood by refilling coffee cups. The tall cups could only be filled halfway to keep the coffee from splashing out due to the vibration of the engine running below deck. Plates danced little jigs on the table in front of the actors as they ate. It was comical to watch them reaching out to grab what they wanted before it got away.

In the kitchen the pots and pans rattled on the shelves and had to be anchored down to keep them from shimmying onto the floor. It got worse when the steamboats passed by, their large waves threw our boats into a rocking fit. It wasn't unusual to see unoccupied chairs scooting across the floor from one side to the other.

Traveling at the average rate of seven miles an hour we continued to wend our way southward along the river. We passed Elizabeth, Pa., where they charged such an exorbitant license fee to show, that it didn't pay us to stop. Chemical plants and steel mills stretched for miles along both sides of the river, giving it the name of "The Steel Capitol of the World."

At the entrance to Lock No. 3 we had to wait in line with several other boats before making passage. Then, when we were back on the river again above the dam, the engine broke down. That brought Dad on the run from the pilothouse.

They tied the boats to a tree and Dad went to work on the engine. It was leaking oil and the cylinder head was cracked. He tried to get gaskets to fit, but they kept burning out. The Jones and Laughlin Steel Mill was on the opposite side of the river, so Marion rowed over there in the skiff to see if they had one that would fit. They didn't, but the plant foreman gave him a bagful of new gasket material with copper sides. Dad custom made a gasket and soon had the engine chugging again.

We rounded the bend, and saw Elrama, a prosperous coal mining town of two thousand population.

The cry "Here comes the showboat," was heard all over town. The townspeople lined the top of the bank in increasing numbers as we drew nearer to the dock.

"Hail, Hail, the Gang's All Here," said the calliope in happy greeting.

One toot of the landing whistle sounded and we began slowing down. Aunt Ida stood at her relay post directing the procedure as before, only in reverse. Dad eased the *Majestic* in to shore and hurried down from the pilothouse, shut off the engine, and helped run out the lines. Then the gangplank was lowered and we were ready for business.

In the meantime the crowd was entertained with more calliope favorites. Soon the Dixieland Jazz Band went uptown to ballyhoo the show. Frank Barton, the hobo clown, was the lead beating on the bass drum. They gave the crowd a sample of their toe tapping music, comedy chatter, and dancing.

Then Samuel Lippencott announced the show and curtain time over the megaphone. He invited them to visit the boat and inspect the new theatre during the afternoon, and reserve their tickets early to get a good seat. Marion and Tommy distributed handbills to the crowd which read:

TONIGHT
MAJESTIC SHOWBOAT
Nicol and Reynolds Newest and Finest Floating Theatre
Launched This Spring At Pittsburgh
– PROUDLY PRESENTS –
THE BLOOMER GIRL
A comedy drama in 4 acts, by A. H. Spinks
Plus 5 vaudeville acts – Plenty of Singing – Dancing –
Comedy – and Music

You liked Our Shows Aboard The *America*. Don't Miss This One!
– ADMISSION PRICES –
Reserved Seats $1.00
Box Seats $1.25
Balcony 75¢
Adult Gen. Admission 50¢
Children Under 12 25¢
Reserved Seats On Sale Aboard The Boat During The Day.
Get Yours Early To Avoid Disappointment. Visitors Welcome.

Showboat people were the celebrities of the day. To meet the performers in person and then watch them on stage was exciting. A visit from the showboat was like a Fourth of July celebration. Something exciting was happening to break the monotony of life in a small town.

During the afternoon a fresh supply of meat, vegetables, ice, and other staples were purchased at the Company Store and delivered to the boat by horse and wagon.

Crowds of people milled on and off the boat all afternoon looking at photographs of the cast, show bills, examining the theatre from all angles, and reserving their tickets for the evening. "No One Allowed On Side Deck" signs were posted on the head of the boat to keep visitors from going upstairs or in back unless they were Dad's special guests.

At 6:30 Frank Cannon presented the first of three calliope concerts prior to the show. He played everything from "Yankee Doodle" to "Where the River Shannon Flows." The music was designed to draw the crowd to the river again and keep them entertained until the doors opened. The longer he played, the more people came.

At 7:30 the *Majestic* lit up like a city setting on the river at twilight and the crowds began filing up the gangplank. Uncle Tegie and Hazel escorted the patrons to their seats down front, while the general admission and balcony patrons helped themselves to the choice seats in their sections.

Every seat in the theatre was filled with happy chattering patrons right back to the last row where I sat next to Mother watching and waiting to see the show.

All became quiet as Uncle Tegie stepped out in front of the curtain. "Good evening, ladies and gentlemen," he said, "On behalf of my partner, Captain Thomas J. Reynolds, the cast, and myself, I take great pleasure in welcoming each and everyone of you on board for our opening night performance. The *Majestic* is a new showboat completed this spring at Pittsburgh. Tonight we are presenting *"The*

Bloomer Girl," plus five vaudeville acts brought straight to you from New York. We are here to entertain you and to see that you have a good time. So sit back, relax, and enjoy yourself. If you like what we do, clap your hands and we'll work all the harder to please you. And now, on with the show. Maestro!" he said, and stepped back in the wings.

The band played "Waiting for the Robert E. Lee," "Way Down Yonder in New Orleans," and "The Basin Street Blues." Then promptly at 8:30 the curtain went up on the show.

The cast: Samuel and Josephine Lippencott; Claude and Mary Clark; Frank and Naomi Barton; Frank Cannon; Uncle Tegie; Dad – a police officer; Marion – mail boy; and Aunt Ida. She was hilarious in her comedy role of the mulatto maid, who shyly sided with the Bloomer Girl in their pursuit of freedom, especially to get them out of hoop skirts. When she yanked up her skirts and showed her red homemade bloomers underneath, it brought the house down.

Between acts of the play were vaudeville acts, slapstick comedy bit "The Mudwhomp" and "School Days" song and dance, by Barton and Barton; a duet "Yes, Sir, That's My Baby," with ukulele accompaniment, by the Clarks; a unicycle act by Sam Lippencott; solo "My Aunt Frances" and Highland fling dance by Hazel Reynolds, in Scottish costume; and a violin solo by Thomas Nicol.

During intermission, peanuts, popcorn, and boxes of Arabian Nights candy were sold at ten cents a box. Each box of candy contained a prize – a small keepsake from the showboat. The prizes included everything from carnival beads, combs, tie clips, and celluloid kewpie dolls, to lucky rabbit feet.

Uncle Tegie strolled out on to stage with his violin. "Everybody works on a showboat. Now, it's my turn," he said. His classical renditions of "Humoresque" and "The Irish Washerwoman" was a big hit.

Finally the curtain rang down on the two-and-one-half-hour performance of song, dance, comedy, and drama.

Uncle Tegie stepped back in front of the curtain and waited for the applause to die down. "Thank you ladies and gentlemen. You have been a wonderful audience and we enjoyed putting on the show for you. Tomorrow night we will be playing Courtney, Pa. If you have friends and relatives there, call them up and tell them about the show. Now, it's time to say goodnight. Watch your step going off the boat. We'll see you again on our return trip downriver. So long everybody," he said.

After the last person moved up the hill and out of sight, Dad hung a lantern signal light on the bow of the *Majestic* and one at the stern of the *Atta Boy* to keep the steamboats from running into us during the night. Then he turned out the theatre lights, doused the fire in the boiler, and came upstairs to bed. One by one all the other lights went out, leaving the boats in inky darkness at the landing. All became blissfully quiet and we slept.

Next morning we headed upriver to Courtney, Pa., four miles away. There the show was presented in its entirety to another capacity crowd of enthusiastic showboatgoers. We made one night stands at Monongahela City, Charoleroi, Belle Vernon, Fayette City, and Bobtown.

In observance of the state Blue Law, we didn't show on Sunday. Except for the work involved in moving the boat and feeding the crew, Sunday was a day of rest and relaxation for us all. We spent the day sightseeing, playing and swimming in the river. Dad swapped river lore with the old timers who came down to the boat. We watched the breathtaking beauty of a gorgeous sunset in different locations every evening.

Aunt Ida did a fine business selling canaries. At the sound of her whistling or Uncle Tegie playing a few bars of "Listen to the Mockingbird" on the violin, the males sang, warbled and chirped at the top of their lungs. She charged $5 each for females, $10 for males, and $15 each for her orange Yorkshire Canaries, a breed from England that was larger than the common canary. She also sold handcrafted cages, cuttlebone, seed, and sand and gravel she scooped up by the bucketsful from sandbars along the river and purified in the oven.

Each day found us moving out of the heavy industrial area and deeper into the coal mining region of the Monongahela Valley. We played towns along both sides of the river in Pennsylvania, then crossed over the state line into West Virginia and hit all the towns in that area.

The river was so crystal clear in places we could see the schools of fish swimming by and boulders and logs deep below the surface of the water.

The mournful wail of steamboat whistles sounded throughout the day and night along the river. If they weren't signalling to pass one another, they were blowing for a landing.

The people of the Monongahela Valley worked hard and played hard. They were very outgoing and demonstrative with their feelings, a delight to the actors. They howled with laughter, stamped their feet and blew wolf whistles every time an actress came on stage. They'd spend their last dollar to see the show.

Fairmont, West Virginia, 127 miles above the mouth of the river, was our last upbound stop. We were booked there for two days. Then we began working our way back downriver.

As we passed Pittsburgh, Aunt Ida told the actresses sitting on the front deck, "Act like ladies. Pull your dresses down over your knees. Don't smoke cigarettes in public. Everybody will be looking at you. Don't shame us."

Women visitors weren't allowed in the pilothouse. It was thought that they would be too distracting to the pilot. But the actors delighted in watching Dad lean back in his chair, arms folded over his chest, steering the boats through boat traffic and under bridges with his feet.

At Stratton, Ohio, we had an addition to the family. Mother took up tickets that night as usual, but around two a.m. she woke Dad. He awakened Aunt Ida, and went uptown with the flashlight to get the doctor. Finding no complications, he sat back and let nature take its course. She gave birth to another daughter around nine o'clock that morning, July 20, 1923.

Dad woke me up and said, "Catherine, you have a baby sister. The stork brought her this morning." Scooping me up in his arms, he carried me into the front room and sat me down on the bed next to Mother and the baby.

"This is Margaret," she said, and held her up for me to see. She was so cute I couldn't take my eyes off her. She looked like a baby doll with her golden curls, blue eyes, and round little face. She was wearing a long white dress with embroidery and tatted lace Mother had made. I touched the palm of her hand with my finger and she closed her tiny fist around it, binding my love for her forever.

St. Mary's, West Virginia, 100 miles further down the Ohio, was a special stop on our itinerary. When we pulled in to the city wharf below Middle Island it was like a homecoming. Half the people there were related to us in one way or another. Our Reynolds ancestors were among the first pioneers to settle the area. Thomas and Mary Ann Edolin Reynolds emigrated from Maryland. They had come over the mountains to Brownsville, Pa., and down the Monongahela and Ohio rivers by raft to St. Marys in 1806. Thomas had traded Jacob LaRue a copper applebutter kettle for fifty acres of land on the lower end of Middle Island.

Using the timber off the land he built a double story log house. Then he set up a logging camp and made a living for himself and twelve children selling logs and railroad ties to the Parkersburg Mill. He was also a soldier in the war of 1812 and had the distinction of being the last veteran of that war in the area.

His son, John Wesley, and Margaret Severs Reynolds were my great-great-grandparents. Their son, Thomas Jefferson Reynolds, and wife Euphemia Dye, were my grandparents.

Dad told me "My grandfather, Thomas, was a mule riding Baptist preacher. He preached wherever he could get a crowd together and kept the peace with his fists."

My grandpa, Marion, was born on the island, February 27,1856. My grandmother, Catherine, was raised in the Shawnee Indian Camp on the Ohio side of the river. Their daughter, Ida, was born in their cabin on Middle Island, July 20, 1885.

Most of the boat landings were owned and maintained by packet companies. The bigger the town, the nicer the landing. Hardly a day went by without our sharing the landing with one or more of the packets running a trade route between Pittsburgh and Cincinnati, Pittsburgh to Marietta, Charleston, W. Va., and Gallipolis, Ohio. They included the four decker *Senator Cordill, J. B. Davis, General Wood, Homer Smith, J. W. Hubbard, East St. Louis, Verne Swain, Greenwood* and the *Tom Green,* that made it's maiden run in 1923, captained by Mrs. Mary B. Greene.

We also shared landings with the Wes Sealy's dish and tinware tradeboat; Ben Raike's Photography Boat; and Doc Bart's Patent Medicine Boat. Where there was a market for a special service or hard to find merchandise, sooner or later a boat would come by to supply it.

At Marietta we entered the 107 mile Muskingum River. Here, everything from the narrow width of the river, to its twelve locks, eleven dams, and five lateral canals built in 1840-1842, was miniature in size compared to the Ohio River.

We made passage through U. S. Lock No. 1, near the mouth of the river and passed through the opened swing-span of the B&O Railroad Bridge. Then, with the actors and yours truly taking in the sights, we wended our way along the tree bordered stream to Devola, for a capacity crowd.

Lowell, our next stop, was a beautiful canal port. The canal was a bypass for boat traffic around the stationary dam on the river. U. S. Lock No. 3 was at the entrance to the canal. The boats had to be uncoupled and locked through one at a time to complete the passage. It was called double lockage. Only one attendant was on call to operate the manual controls and oversee the lockages. Dad, Uncle Tegie, and the boys gave him a hand and tended the boats. They pulled the *Majestic* into the chamber, with only a few inches to spare along the sides. As soon as she completed lockage, having been lifted fifteen feet to the upper pool inside the canal, the flood water was released from the chamber and the *Atta Boy* locked through.

People watched us from the front porches of their lovely old homes and from the banks of the canal as we passed by with calliope playing. There were no mournful steamboat whistles blowing along the river or other boats passing by to disturb the performance that evening.

Next morning we moved on to Beverly, Ohio, another canal town with U. S. Lock 4 at the entrance. We made another double lockage and moved through the canal. That evening the river road was lined with people coming on foot, horseback, and by the wagon loads to fill the theatre.

At Dad's request everybody was up, dressed and forewarned about the danger that awaited us at the head of the canal when we left the following morning. There we had to make a left turn out of the narrow exit, directly in front of the menacing looking dam to get back out on the Muskingum. It was scary as we came closer and closer to the top of the dam and emerged from the exit. But, with the help of a line holding us in tow, and Dad at the helm, we made it and continued on our way to the next town.

There was very little boat traffic on the Muskingum. Once in a while we passed a small gasboat in tow of a mussel barge, a sand and gravel scow or a coal barge. Family houseboats tied up along the banks in the shade of overhanging tree branches, and fishermen were common sights. They were sitting along the riverbanks fishing with cane poles and cork stoppers, or in johnboats tending their nets, trotlines, and fishing for mussels.

Slowing our pace, Dad would invariably call out from the pilothouse window and ask the first fisherman he saw, "Are the fish biting?" If they were, the fishermen held up a large catfish for him to see. "What are you using for bait?" Dad would ask. Whatever it was, sour dough balls, chicken entrails, crawfish, or worms, that's what he and the boys used to bait the trotline they set out at the towns. They fished for the fun of it as well as for the table. Catfish weighing up to thirty pounds were taken on trotlines, and larger ones in nets. Fried, breaded catfish was an everyday part of our menu while we toured the little river.

We showed at Stockport, McConnelsville, and Malta. At Malta we laid dangerously close to the top of the dam. Then on to Eagelport, Gaysport, and Philo, the last stop. It was 66.8 miles above the mouth of the Muskingum.

Then, changing over to an alternate play, *"Fighting for Honor,"* we worked our way back down out of the Muskingum and up the Ohio River to Pittsburgh. There we continued upbound on the Monongahela River and revisited towns with a top notch Musical Revue.

Too soon the warm days of summer had turned into fall. It was too chilly to go in swimming. Heat had to be turned on in the theatre, and the stoves fired up in our rooms. Then there was snow on the ground and soon the river would be freezing over. The traveling showboat was a warm weather operation. On a cold blustery evening in early November, the final curtain rang down on the show. We said goodbye to the actors and actresses who had become our good friends and returned to Glenwood for the winter. Thus ending our first tour with the *Majestic*.

Chapter 4
Wintertime Aboard the Showboat

All the special equipment used aboard the boat during the tour was stored away for use again next season. The theatre, staterooms, company kitchen and dining room were locked up. Then Uncle Tegie, Aunt Ida, Mom, Dad, and the five children settled down to wintertime living in our apartments. We literally holed up in a wonderful world of our own, aboard the boat.

There were no mortgage payments to be met, no mooring charge for use of the landing, and no utility bills to pay. Our drinking water came from a watermain on the riverbank. Fuel coal was picked up along the railroad tracks where it had fallen off fast moving freight cars. Our electricity came from a generator aboard the *Atta Boy*. We had our own storehouse, so very few trips had to be made to the grocery store.

Like a farmer's wife, Mother canned everything she could get her hands on during the summer and stored it in the hull beneath the backstage. She put up hundreds of jars of blackberrys, raspberries, vegetables, sauces, pickles, relishes, applebutter, jellies, beef, chicken, pigs' feet, tongue and tails. You name it and she had a jarful of it setting on the shelves for quick fixings.

Dad made a round of the wholesale houses and stocked the stateroom on the lower front deck with virtually everything else in bulk quantities that we'd need. We had fresh fruit, potatoes, condensed milk, flour, coffee, dried beans and a 300 pound freshly dressed pork preserved in salt. There was chewing tobacco for Dad, sewing notions for mother, and a variety of home medical remedies.

Whenever we needed something from the store all we had to do was to to the front of the boat and get it.

Dad set aside the usual $500 to tide us through the winter. Barring an emergency, very little of it would have to be spent.

The sights and sounds of the city were all around us. Smog hovered over the valley during the day and the city lights illuminated it at night. Trolley cars making "The Loop" between downtown Pittsburgh and Glenwood clanged for stops on half hour intervals at the foot of the bridge spanning the river below the boats. Passenger trains moved in and out of the Downtown and Glenwood Station underneath the highway bridge. Freight trains hauling coal rumbled past the showboat all hours of the day and night. There were steamboats, packets, and other craft moving in and out of the river and stopping at the city wharf.

The happiest time was when Grandpa and Uncle Bill brought the *America* in for the winter after closing the show. They landed the showboat bow to bow with the *Majestic* and ran out the gangplank next to ours. That way we were like one big family. When we wanted to visit all we had to do was hop over the fence railings.

What a wonderful time it was Dad and Aunt Ida to be with the father and brother they adored, Mother with her sister, and the kids with our four double cousins. Their ages were nearly the same as ours. Marion and Bill, Jr., Hazel and Ida Mae, Tommy and Raymond, went to school in town and played together. Frank (Buddy) was my favorite friend. As I recall, I wasn't very nice to him sometimes. Because of my affliction I couldn't run and play with him and we ended up fighting. I sent him home crying with scratches on his face nearly every time he came to visit. But thinking it might help cheer me up, Aunt Fan sent him back, and I'd scratch him again. Everybody catered to me in one way or another. I was a spoiled brat.

Grandpa, who remained a widower after his second wife died, lived in the room where I was born on the back deck of the *America*. Dad would take me there to visit. We sat in chairs by the crackling fire and grandpa gave me a stick of licorice candy and Dad a tincup full of apple cider. Grandpa was an avid fisherman, hunter, and trapper, and his room reflected his interest. Cone shaped fish nets he had hand knitted himself, dip nets, trotlines, cane poles, and steel muskrat traps hung from the rafters. There was a gun rack on the wall. He loved to hunt rabbits, squirrels, ducks, geese, and turkeys. He killed muskrats to keep them from gnawing holes in the boats' hulls. Of course he sold the hides.

He also had dried fruit and ears of popcorn strung up along the wall. Baskets of fruit and nuts he'd gathered from the woods sat around the room for snacks. There was a jug of applejack when he wanted a drink.

He was a whiz at beating the boys playing dominoes and checkers. Occasionally he had some of his old cronies in for an all night poker game. While on tour with the *America* he had served as co-pilot, engineer, deckhand, sold tickets, and helped handle business affairs.

Uncle Bill and family lived on the front of the *America*. A happy-go-lucky person, he was the extreme opposite of Dad in every way. He was six feet and four inches tall, skinny as a rail, had black hair, and a glass eye.

He was one day old when the houseboat he was born on settled down on a stump and sank during the night when the river fell. The family was awakened by the water rising up over their bed, and by the time they reached shore they were freezing wet. Uncle Bill got an infection in his right eye and when he was four days old, his eye had to be removed.

In spite of his handicap he excelled as master pilot, general manager, and press agent for the *America*. He spared no expense in producing the shows and advertising the showboat. He was also a fine actor. He co-directed the shows, sang and danced, and was a good comedian. He'd come on stage looking at the audience with his one eye and say, "Well, here I am . . . Just what you've been waiting for, a long drink of water!" Soon he'd have them rolling in the aisles with laughter.

He was also a born musician. He loved music and could play a tune on everything from an ordinary comb, carpenters saw with a violin bow, to the piano and calliope. You'd see him sitting off to himself gazing into space playing a sentimental ballad on the harmonica, sweet potato, ukulele, or concertina. Sometimes he played hoe down music on the banjo and Dixieland jazz on the trumpet.

Dad and Uncle Bill weren't idle for very long that winter. They were offered good paying jobs for the use of the *Atta Boy* and *Liberty* towboats and their piloting services to transport sand and gravel for a dredging company in operation upriver from Glewnwood.

Leaving at daybreak they made a number of trips past the showboats with sand and gravel scows to the unloading docks and returned with empties to the dredging site for refilling. I remember sitting by the window watching for Dad. He tooted the whistle to let me know he was coming and we'd wave to each other as he went by.

Aunt Ida kicked off her Christmas bird sale aboard the boat. Her ad in the *Pittsburgh Press* brought a number of customers. She had a special pet canary, a yellow male, that could whistle the tune to "Dixie." She had spent two years training him and she was asked to exhibit him at the World's Fair.

She sold the birds, reserving her choice breeding stock and left them in mother's care. Then, wearing a black satin coat with monkey fur trim, perky hat, and carrying Queenie on her arm, she and Tegie left on their annual trip to Chicago and New Orleans for the horse races.

Christmas was a time of joy and expectation. A pine tree from the woods was set in front of the living room window overlooking the river. I helped make paper chains to decorate the tree. We had tinsel, store bought ornaments, candles, and a silver star on the top. Each of the children hung up one long black stocking on Christmas Eve and awoke next morning to find it brimful of candy, fruit, and nuts. There was also a hobbyhorse with special leg exercisers for me, a doll baby for Margaret, a sled for Tommy, and ice skates for Marion and Hazel. It wasn't long until our cousins came running to show us the gifts they'd received from Santa Claus.

Below zero temperature and blinding snowstorms made shore ice build up around the boats, freezing them in solid at the landing. Every morning and evening after returning from work with the towboats, Dad, Grandpa, and Uncle Bill got out on the ice with axes and handsaws and cut the ice away from the boats' hulls. The frequent traveling of boats with their barge tows kept the channel open. Then, as conditions worsened, hampering navigation, Dad quit the towing job and hired on as a boat carpenter at the Morgan Davis Dock Company at Hazelwood for the duration of the winter.

On cold wintery evenings he liked to listen over the earphones to the radio or sit in his favorite rocking chair by the crackling fire and play the violin. Though he wasn't a trained musician like Uncle Tegie, he had a good ear for songs he heard and played them with heart and soul. "Turkey in the Straw, Pop Goes the Weasel, Hand Me Down My Walking Cane, Chicken Reel, Red Wing, Down by the Riverside," and "Maggie," were his favorites.

Someone was always dropping in at our place. If it wasn't Grandpa, my aunts and uncles, it was our cousins coming to play. What a houseful of noisemakers we were. When the kids got too rambunctious, Dad had Hazel and Ida Mae do their singing and dancing specialties they'd performed on stage during the summer. Sometimes the boys sang while Dad played the accompaniment on the violin. It was like a party with Mother serving hot cocoa and popcorn.

Let the snow fly, let the river freeze over, Monday was wash day. It was a major operation for Mother drawing water from the river through a hole cut in the ice and heating it in tubs on the cookstove. Using a bar of her homemade lye soap, she scrubbed the white clothes on the board. Those with stubborn stains were boiled in the copper boiler and washed through again until spotlessly clean. Then she hung the clothes out on the back, deck to freeze dry and pressed everything with a flat irons the next day.

Saturday was bath day, come what may. Mother saw to that. The washtub was filled with warm water and curtained off in the corner by the cook stove. One by one, everybody from Dad down had to strip off their clothes and take a turn in the tub.

Then, if we weren't snowed in, Dad took us on the trolley to downtown Pittsburgh to see a moving picture or vaudeville show. We alternated going to the Bijou, Harris, or Nixon Theatre, where big name stars of the day headed the bill.

Dad was casually dressed the first time he took us to the ritzy Nixon Theatre and they wouldn't let us in. He wasn't wearing a necktie. We waited in line until he went to a nearby store and bought a tie. We enjoyed the entertainment and picked up new ideas to use in our own show next season.

Aunt Fan, Mother's sister, was full of fun and liked to tease and play with all the kids. Unlike Mother, who never acted on stage, Aunt Fan was a talented actress. She performed character parts in dramas, and sang and danced in the vaudeville lineups aboard the *America*. She also helped manage business affairs, took up tickets, and cooked for the family and actors.

Mother, who liked to work with her hands, created beautiful and practical things with needle and thread. She made nearly all of our clothing. Nothing was wasted. She would cut down Dad's old serge pants and suits for Marion, and when he outgrew them she'd cut them down again to fit Tommy. She kept bolts of cloth on hand and could make any article of clothing or costumes for the show, with or without a pattern. She could look at a picture in a fashion magazine and make the entire ensemble for herself. She was a fine seamstress. Her work could be seen everywhere, in the actor's staterooms, our quarters, on stage, and on our backs.

The spring thaw sent water surging down the mountain ravines, rivers, and creeks into the Monongahela building up to an ice run.

"The Monongahela's busted loose!" "The Monongahela's busted loose!" The cry was heard all up and down the river, and over the radio, warning boatmen of impending danger. Every precaution was taken to safeguard property against the oncoming destruction. The ice run was capable of wrecking and sinking the boats with one blow.

Soon the river was running brimful of ice, refuse, and flotilla caught up in the floe. Logs, uprooted trees, railroad ties, lumber, unopened crates of merchandise from warehouses near the river, and ill-fated crafts of all sizes swept past the showboats.

We could feel the boats listing and straining at their moorings under the grinding impact. The ice rammed and scraped against the hulls as it went by. Only the children closed their eyes and slept during the ice run. Though my family was used to it, they were alert and ready to spring into action in an emergency.

After we came safely through another ice run, Aunt Ida always said, "The luck of the Irish was with us, begorra!"

Marion left school a few weeks early to help spruce up the *Majestic* and *Atta Boy*. They were covered with layers of soot and grit. Using brooms, scrub brushes, and lye they scrubbed the showboat and towboat from stem to stern, then gave them a new coat of paint.

Our ad for actors appeared in the February 23, 1924 issue of the *Billboard*. It read:

"*Showboat Majestic Wants* - Dramatic and vaudeville people. Parts and specialties. Six shows a week, two bills a season. If double piano advise. Easiest and surest money in show business. Like a vacation. Newest and safest boat on the river. Operated by experienced owners. No kids or pets. State age, height, weight, and lowest in first. Address: Nicol & Reynolds, Hazelwood Station, Pittsburgh, Pa."

Five of the actors who toured with us aboard the *Majestic* the previous season were hired over other applicants. They were Samuel and Josephine Lippencott, Claude and Mary Clark, and Frank Cannon. Mr. and Mrs. Harry Mock were newcomers to the showboat circuit.

Uncle Bill also spruced up the *America* and hired seven actors via his ad in the March 1st edition of *Billboard*:

"Wanted - Dramatic people with vaudeville specialties, or vaudeville people that can do parts. Thirty-two weeks for the right people. One show a day, three bills per season. A regular summer vacation. The show opens April 1st. No tickets unless I know you. Leave your pets and babies at home. Everything paid after joining. William Reynolds, Care *America Showboat,* Hazelwood Station, Pittsburgh, Pa."

April 1st, 1924, both the *America* and *Majestic* left Glenwood and headed out on their summer tours.

Chapter 5
Heyday of the Showboats
1924

There was an old saying that "Spring officially arrived when the first strains of the callliope could be heard along the river and the first showboat of the season pulled into the landing."

So spring busted out all over when we stopped at Elrama, Pennsylvania with calliope playing, people running to the riverbank to watch, and the Dixieland Band ballyhooing the show uptown.

The three act comedy drama, *"Her Midnight Guest,"* plus five acts of vaudeville was the opening night presentation. They were, "School Days," singing and dancing by Clark and Clark; a violin solo by Thomas Nicol; "The Sidewalks of New York," solo and waltz clog dance, by Hazel Reynolds; chair balancing and juggling exposition, by Lippencott and Lippencott; and "The Ransome," a comedy bit about a cat that got his tail caught in the sewing machine, singing and eccentric dancing by Mock and Mock.

From there we continued upbound on the Monongahela River to Fairmont, W. Va. The play *"The Balloon Girl"* was presented along with a change of vaudeville specialties on our return trip.

Then we headed south on the Ohio River. All went well until two of the actresses got into a fight backstage while the show was going on. One was angry with the other for flirting with her husband and hit her over the head with an iron. She had been pressing clothes between her scenes in the play. The yelling, screaming, and name calling that followed could be heard out front above the actors' voices on stage. By the time Dad arrived to break it up, their husbands had joined in the fight. Dad fired all four of them and gave them two weeks notice to pack up and leave. The other actors jumped the show, sympathizing with those fired.

Five new actors were hired via a quick ad in the *Billboard* which read:

> "*Majestic Showboat* wants dramatic people with specialties, or vaudeville people that do parts; General business team and straight man and ingenue, people in other lines. If double piano advise. No kids or dogs. State lowest in first. We pay all after joining. Newest and safest boat on the river. Louisa, Ky., July 9th and 10th, Prichard, W. Va., 11th, White Creek, Ky., 12th, Cattlettsburgh, Ky., 13 and 14th, Russel, Ky., 15th. Address "Nicol and Reynolds.

The new actors hired were Mr. and Mrs. Charles Bates, Mr. and Mrs. Eddie Snyder, and Billy Groves. Uncle Tegie threw a coniption fit when the Snyders arrived leading a painted pony.

"For crimmney sakes," he exploded. "They're bringing a live pony! I thought they used a pony costume in their act. For two cents I'd send them right back where they came from and hire another team in their place."

"Don't be so hasty. That would take time and set us back in our billing. They're a fine looking team. Let's meet them and see what the pony can do," Dad said.

"All right," Uncle Tegie reluctantly agreed. "But where will we put the pony if we decide to let them stay?"

"On the back deck. There's room under the stairway to build a stall and we can keep it washed off with the fire hose," Dad replied.

The animal, named Pony Boy, was led up the gangplank onto the front deck and lifted his leg on command to shake hands with Dad and Uncle Tegie, breaking the ice and bringing broad grins to their faces.

"What else can he do?" Uncle Tegie asked.

"Anything I want him to do," Mr. Snyder said, and began putting the pony through it's paces. Counting up to ten with his hoof on the deck, shaking his head yes and no to the questions asked him, waltzing, doing the two-step, and other circus tricks.

"How would Pony Boy be at helping ballyhoo the show uptown?" Uncle Tegie asked.

"Great. He'd love it," Mr. Snyder said, sewing up the job and adding a whole new dimension to our program.

Uncle Bill changed actors several times before he got the show he wanted. His last ad in the July 12the issue of *Billboard* read:

> "*Wanted Showboat America* - General business team with specialties that can play leads. Professionals with wardrobes, not amateurs with suitcases. Misrepresentation cause of my last three ads. Will send tickets, but tell

the truth. State all in first. One show per day, two bills to get up in. Money sure. Lowel, Ohio, July 9th, Little Hocking, Ohio, 10th, Reedsville, 11th, Ravenswood, W. Va. 12th, Millwood 13 and 14th, Letart, 15th, after that Point Pleasant, W. Va.

The following writeup by George Peddington, *Billboard* Repertoire Editor, gives an insight into the kind of shows he put on and the kind of showman Uncle Bill was.

"Presentation on the *America* Thrills - Reynolds Players Delight Folks of Constance, Ky, with Western Play.

Accepting an invitation to visit the showboat *America*, owned and managed by Wm. Reynolds, the editor was delightfully entertained Monday night, August 25, when he witnessed the performance of the Reynolds Players in a four act play, *"The Weasel,"* at Constance, Ky.

As we approached the boat a steam calliope was heard. Gay colored lights on the showboat were welcoming at what would otherwise have been a lonely spot on the riverbank.

Mr. Reynolds accommodatingly showed us around the boat. We found very comfortable quarters on the upper deck where the Reynolds family and other members of the cast make their home. There are seven living rooms on the boat and below is the theatre 80 x 20, with a fair sized stage equipped with good looking scenery and the best in props. The theatre seats 300. The boat itself is 100 x 20 feet.

Before the curtain went up at 8:35 we glanced at the audience. It was an enthusiastic crowd before the play and after the final curtain. Some had come from distant points back in the hills of Kentucky. Others were from Constance, the little river town. It had been some time since a showboat anchored in their vicinity; they were starved for a pinch of drama, and comedy, for a thriller a la westerner. Judging by their wholehearted, spontaneous applause repeatedly during the show. It was evidence beyond contradiction that they were happy and receiving their money's worth.

Piano and snaredrum music opened the show. Then lights flicked. It was the cue for silence. The curtain went up and the plot unfolded.

Mr. Reynolds gave a good performance in the part of the tall, lean westerner, known as Uncle Duddley. Mrs.

Harry Van, as the "Widder" played her role with true characterization and handled her comedy lines well. As the villain, Hercher Wiles put forth the heavy lines across in utmost satisfaction of all. There was the "Dutch" comedian, Hans, capably played by Harry Van. Mary, pretty girl of the story, creditably handled by Mrs. Harry Van. The sheriff, commendably acted by Harry Van. The plot was clean and enjoyable. The only objectionables were an occasional damn.

Then comes a vaudeville specialty by Mr. Wiles, who proves even a villain can be nice before the footlights. His song titled "When Rose Blows Her Nose Her Hose Shows" scores. Ida Mae Reynolds, followed with a nifty specialty dance for a girl of ten. Her red dress was pretty.

Mr. and Mrs. Vine did a song and dance specialty. Their presentation of "Momma Loves Poppa" went across for a big hand.

After Act 3, Mrs. Vine then appears in a comedy song number in which she delights the audience by joshing the men folks down front.

Act four winds up the plot.

Others living on the boats besides the actors and Mr. and Mrs. Reynolds are Marion Reynolds, William's father, who is ticketseller, Bill Reynolds, Jr. fireman, and Tom Tenant, breakman."

Seventeen showboats plied the Ohio River and it's tributaries the summer of 1924.

D. Otto Hitner's *Cotton Blossom No. 1,* in tow of the steamboat *Grace Devers.* Launched that spring it was the newest and largest drama and vaudeville showboat on the river. Seating capacity 1,400 people.

Golden Rod, in tow of the steamboat *Crown Hill.* Owned and operated by Capt. John "Bill" Menke and his brothers Harry, Charles and Ben Menke. Seating capacity 1,000. Billed "The World's Greatest Showboat – The Best in Drama – Vaudeville and Music."

French's New Sensation, in tow of the former packet steamer *Chaperon,* owned and operated by the Menke Brothers. Built in 1901, it seated 700. A musical show, augmented by six chorus girls in line, and band was featured.

The New Sunny South, drama and vaudeville showboat, in tow of the twin-wheeled gasboat *Lucy Coles.* Owned and operated by James Bonnelli and Capt. E. P. Mathews. Built in 1922, it seated 450.

The Water Queen, drama and vaudeville showboat, in tow of the former packet steamer *Argand.* Owned and operated by Capt. Roy Hyatt and his wife Josephine. Built in 1889, it was the oldest showboat on the river. Seated 624.

Bryant's, drama and vaudeville showboat, in tow of the former Muskingum River packet *Valley Belle.* Owned and operated by Samuel and Capt. Billy Bryant family, it was built in 1917 and seated 700.

Columbia, drama and vaudeville showboat, in tow of the steamboat *J. M. Grubbs.* Owned and operated by Capt. Steven Price and his father Edwin Price, it was built in 1911 and seated 650 people.

Princess, drama and vaudeville showboat, in tow of the gasboat *Florence.* Norman Thom was owner and operator. Built in 1907, it seated 200 and was billed "A Small Showboat – But a Big Show."

Water Lily, moving picture and vaudeville showboat, in tow of the gasboat *Margaret R.* was owned and operated by The Farnsworth and Lunzel Enterprises. Built in 1918, it seated 200.

River Maid, drama and vaudeville showboat, owned and operated by Capt. Hi and family was built in 1918 and seated 300.

Valley, in tow of the gasboat *Edna M.,* was owned and operated by the Harry Hart family. A minstrel show was alternately presented with drama and vaudeville during the season. Built in 1918, it seated 400.

Gaity, moving picture and vaudeville showboat, owned and operated by the William Hart family, seated 200 people.

Rex, moving picture showboat, owned and operated by F. B. Potts was built in 1921 and had a 400 seating capacity.

Marge, moving picture and vaudeville showboat was the smallest showboat on the river. It was a motor launch converted into a 50-seat theatre, owned and operated by the A. J. Wiles family.

The Floating Playhouse, owned and operated by Capt. Ralph Waldo (Gaches) Emerson, featured a vaudeville stage show and jazz band. Seating capacity was 900.

America Showboat, built by T. J. Reynolds and Thomas Nicol, operated by William and Marion Reynolds, in tow of the *Liberty.* Built in 1917, seated 300.

Majestic Showboat, in tow of the *Atta Boy,* built, owned and operated by Thomas J. Reynolds and Thomas Nicol. Built in 1923, seated 425.

Every now and then we'd pass one of the other showboats. We'd all stop what we were doing and hurry on deck to watch. We were happy to see one another, like family. Dad and the other captains exchanged friendly greetings from the pilothouse, and the first one to the calliope greated the other with a snappy tune. Then soon as the last chord sounded, the other calliopist picked up playing as they passed by.

One day, shortly after our arrival in a small town, the *America* came with the Dixieland Jazz Band on the top deck playing for us. What a beautiful sight! Grandpa was in the pilothouse and Uncle Bill was leading the band playing the trumpet. Dressed in red and white candy striped jackets, white pants and straw hats, they made the valley rock with their toe tapping songs, "Waiting for the Robert E. Lee, Ja Da, Sugar Blues," and "Basin Street Blues."

Grandpa landed the *America* alongside our showboat for a visit before going on to the next town. No sooner had the boats come together than over the fence railing came Aunt Fan, Ida Mae and Frank, giving us bear hugs. The actors also got together and we all caught up on the news.

Uncle Bill said Ida Mae was scoring big with her singing and dancing specialty "The Charleston." One night he forgot the words to a song, "The Green Grass Grew All Around." He was using a broom for a prop and kept going around it trying to think of the words. Finally, he looked at the audience with his one eye, and told them, "Aw, the hell with it!" and went offstage. But they demanded an encore, and when he went back, he did it right!

There were days at a time when we didn't see any other showboats and had the business all to ourselves. There were other times they were so close playing adjoining towns that we could hear their calliopes. It wasn't unusual for us to pull into a landing just vacated by a showboat playing the night before. Occasionally due to a mix-up in billing, we double dated an engagement at a town with another showboat. If it was big enough to support two showboats at the same time, we were sure of getting large crowds. But if it wasn't, the first boat at the landing stayed and the other one moved on to wildcat the next town. Sometimes they both stayed and competed with one another for business.

Smithland, Kentucky was our last downbound stop. The town lies on a high bluff overlooking the Ohio, at the junction of the Cumberland River, 920.5 miles from Pittsburgh.

Shortly after our arrival the big *Cotton Blossom Showboat* came down the Ohio with calliope playing, and instead of passing by, she pulled into the landing with her broad bow facing ours and ran out the gangplank.

"For Pete's sake!" Uncle Tegie exploded. "We can't compete with a boat like that. The town isn't big enough for the two of us. I think we should move to another town and let Hitner have it."

"I don't. We were billed in the town and here first," Dad calmly replied.

"You know we don't stand a snowball of a chance in hell of getting a crowd," Tegie replied.,

"Maybe not, but it will be a lot of fun trying," Dad said.

"All right," Uncle Tegie gave in. "But you mark my words, we won't show tonight!"

Like Captain Ralph Emerson's showboat slogan: "After the Minnow Comes the Whale," and us looking like the minnow lying next to the *Cotton Blossom,* we continued as scheduled there.

With everybody leaving the levee to watch, our little band of actors went uptown with Pony Boy and ballyhooed the show.

Then Hitner's fifteen piece band, looking handsome in their blue and white uniforms, presented a concert in the town square.

Playing host to two beautiful new showboats, especially one the size of the *Cotton Blossom,* created quite a bit of excitement at the town. Men, women, and children milled on and off our boat and the *Cotton Blossom.*

As Dad often did when we were within walking or rowing distance of another showboat, he took me with him to see the *Cotton Blossom.* Captain Hitner met us as we went on board and took us on a grand tour of the showboat and towboat, *Grace Devers.* We ended up in front of cages full of spider monkeys, bobcats, raccoons, parrots and canaries on the upper deck of the *Grace Devers,* which was a converted packet.

That evening it was a battle of calliopes for the favor of the crowd down by the riverside. Peggy Snyder, our calliopist, and the *Cotton Blossom's,* kept the music flowing one after the other. People came from both sides of the river to listen to the music and wait for the show. Then came the clincher.

Before the lights came on, as the sun dipped down behind the hills, the band presented a rousing concert. Everybody began filing up the gangplank . . . aboard the *Cotton Blossom.*

Our spotlight also pointed the way to our gangplank. By curtain time not a single, solitary person bought a ticket to see our show. For the first time we blacked out. So, we all went to the show aboard the *Cotton Blossom* as guests of the Hitners.

Next morning we headed upbound on the Cumberland River, 309 miles in length. For the first part, the river was still in it's natural state. Like all rivers we traveled it was the life flow of the towns and a highway flowing past their front doors to the world outside. The people were dependent on the Paducah to Nashville packet, *Tennessee,* for commercial exchange and travel.

Every morning found us moving a little farther inland on the river. It was partially obstructed in places by dangerous shoals and rock formations. Occasionally we'd pull over next to the bank to make room for a gasboat with a long string of logs to pass by.

Most towns had a boat landing. In some of the out-of-the-way places we stopped, the only signs of people living there was a wagon path leading down through the corn fields to the river. Sometimes there was a self-serve ferry. But Dad knew there were people back in the hills, and come evening at the sound of the calliope playing, here they came on horseback and by the wagonloads to see the show.

Old timers delighted in coming down to the boat during the day and swapping river lore with Dad. When they left, he knew every showboat that had stopped there in the last ten years, and the kind of shows they had put on.

It was common practice for farmers to bring us a bushel basketful of sweet corn, green beans or tomatoes from their garden. They would never let Dad pay for them, as they were just "being neighborly."

Occasionally, we played a town where a protracted religious meeting was going on. No matter what denomination it was, Mother never missed an opportunity going. If it was a week night, she waited until all the patrons were seated in the theatre, then took Margaret and me with her to the church. Being a lot like the pioneer women in the congregation she made friends easily. They would all be down to the boat to see her, and the show, when we stopped there again on our return trip downriver.

We played all the towns in Kentucky between Dycusburgh and Linton, then crossed over the Tennessee state line and played all the way to Nashville.

On our way back downriver we presented the alternate bill, *"Her Midnight Guest."* From the time we had entered the Cumberland River, we had dropped out of sight and the public eye. To let everybody know our whereabouts and the kind of business we were doing, the following is a letter Uncle Tegie sent to *Billboard* for the October 25, 1924 edition:

> "Thomas Nicol, manager of the *Majestic Showboat,* states a route on the Cumberland River is now being followed. We are enjoying beautiful weather and doing a nice business. The company has been presenting the *"Balloon Girl,"* a Robert Sherman play, which is pleasing all classes of people. The roster includes Mr. and Mrs. Charles Bates, characters and specialties; Billy Groves and Dorothy Church, general business man and lady, with singing and double musical specialty; Mr. and Mrs. Eddie Snyder, comedian and soubrette with dancing specialties; Casper Lynn, general business and specialty; Little Hazel Reynolds, song and dance specialty; and Tegie Nicol's heavies.

In the pit is a five piece orchestra, with Mr. Nicol
violinist; Groves, cornetists; Lynn, saxophonist; Miss Church,
trap drums, and Peggy Snyder, pianist and director."

It was also at this time we received news of the loss of William
Hart's *Gaity Showboat*. It was destroyed by fire at Pittsburgh. Mr.
Hart, his wife, son Robert and his wife Mary, and small daughter,
Violet, were alone on the boat when the fire originated in the
projection booth. Mary leaped off the boat with the baby in her arms.
Mrs. Hart remembered to get the money they'd saved from a trunk
before leaving the boat. The loss of this popular boat reduced our
number to sixteen and started the gradual decline of the old-time
floating theatres.

At Eddyville we were held up for ten days due to lengthy repairs
on the locks. Grandpa and Uncle Bill, who had made the tour to
Nashville ahead of us with the *America*, were also there with other
boats tied up along the shore waiting to make passage.

Back on the Ohio we finished out the remainder of the season.
Then we went into winter harbor at Point Pleasant, W. Va.

From the time we opened the show the first of April, until we tied
up at Point Pleasant in mid-November, we had traveled 2,500 miles
touring the Monongahela, Ohio, and Cumberland Rivers. We visited
over 200 towns in seven states: Pennsylvania, West Virginia, Ohio,
Kentucky, Indiana, Illinois, and Tennessee. We had entertained over
80,000 people.

By this time all the showboats had gone into winter harbor.
Bryant's at Elizabeth, Pa., *Floating Playhouse* at Pittsburgh, *Water
Queen* and *Princess* in the lock canal at Lowel, Ohio, *Goldenrod* and
French's Sensation at Paducah, Ky., *Columbia* and *Cotton Blossom*
at Spottsville, Ky., and the *New Sunny South, Water Lily, River
Maid, Valley, Rex, Marge, America*, and *Majestic* at the mouth of the
Kanawha River at Point Pleasant, W. Va.

Some of the showboat operators left their boats in charge of a
caretaker and led interesting lives away from the river in the winter.
The James Bonnelli family took to the road with a minstrel show and
played the deep south until time to go on tour with the showboat
again. The Bryant family took their stage show to Broadway; Otto
Hitner operated a Real Estate business in St. Petersburg, Florida;
Roy and Josephine Hyatt retired to their winter home in Kissimmee,
Florida, where they owned an orange grove. Horses and horse racing
being their passion, Uncle Tegie and Aunt Ida left on their annual trip
to Chicago and New Orleans.

When the rivers froze, a man from Henderson drove his Model
T Ford across the mouth of the Kanawha River, between Stone's ferry

landing, to prove how thick the ice was. Skaters, young and old alike, including Dad, Hazel, Ida Mae, and all the boys, had a wonderful time playing on the ice. Up one side and down the other, they skated past the showboats, steamboats, and other crafts tied up along the banks. Round and round they went enjoying the winter sport until the spring rains set in.

Then came the dreaded ice run. Hundreds of miles of raging floodwater and rending ice packs and jams barreled down on us from the Kanawha and its headwaters and emptied into the ice filled Ohio River. Day after day the ice kept coming and bombarding us with timber-shattering impact, threatening to tear us loose from the landing.

The evening of the peak of the ice run, which was expected to be the worst in years, Mother, Aunt Ida, and Fan took the girls and Frank, two poodle dogs, a cageful of canaries, and personal belongings to Neal's Grocery Store. It was open to anyone off the boats in harbor needing a safe place to stay during the night. There were several other mothers there with their children, pets, and baggage. People continued to come as the conditions worsened.

Mr. Neal, a deacon in the church we attended, lived upstairs over the store with his wife and daughters. They brought in chairs and blankets and did everything they could do to make us comfortable. I remember sitting by the brine pickle barrel and helping myself to a couple of pickles. I don't think I slept any, I was too busy listening and watching everything that was going on. The children slept on the floor while the adults talked in low voices and slouched in their chairs catnapping. The people coming into the store during the night kept us informed of the damage the ice had wrought. Barges and boats were swept loose from their moorings, wrecked, overturned, and carried down out of the river in the ice floe. One couple narrowly escaped with their lives when their houseboat was pulled loose and they leaped ashore with their two young children in their arms.

In the morning we gathered up our belongings and headed back home. You can imagine how happy we were to see the boats were still there. Though the ice would run its course for several more days, the showboats were saved to make another tour.

That winter, Dad and Uncle Tegie helped Grandpa and Uncle Bill build a larger towboat for the *America* Showboat. The new towboat was the same size of the *Atta Boy* and was named *Ida Mae* for my aunt and cousin. They also installed a 32 note calliope and a 60hp engine, and she was ready to travel.

This brought the number of showboats, towboats, etc., they had built to ten. Still seaworthy, the *Liberty* gasboat was sold for $15.

Chapter 6
Footlight Fantasies
and Real Life Drama

We opened the season at Glenwood, West Virginia April 2, 1925, and continued south on the Ohio River playing towns en route to the Green River.

The *Billboard* Repertoire Editor had this to say about our performance:

"SPLENDID PERFORMANCE OF THE CRIMSON NEMISIS AT NORTH BEND, OHIO ... The editor of this department was the guest of Messrs. Nicol and Reynolds, managers of the showboat *Majestic*, at North Bend, Ohio, Monday night, April 20, and witnessed the company's presentation of the *"Crimson Nemesis."* The theatre was well filled and the audience expressed keen appreciation of the drama and the accompanying vaudeville specialties. The *Majestic's* cast is a good one. The character work, of John Hasner is especially to be commended and the work of Dolly LaMarr. Frank "Rusty" Barton, Sam Lippencott, Violet Witt and Royal Ellwood also is excellent. Thomas Reynolds and Thomas Nicol also have small parts as police officers.

The vaudeville between acts pleased immensely, each number going over big. Baby Hazel entertained with some cute songs and dances. Hassner and Witt did a humorous man and wife bit. Frank Barton delighted with his monologue, "Dew Drop Inn," done in blackface. The last act introduced the Great Ellwood in a clever ventrilo-

quist bit. Nicol and Reynolds are to be complimented on
the good show they have this season."

Next morning we passed Cincinnati. Packets were lined up in a
row at the city wharf dispersing passengers and freight. The excursion steamers *Island Belle, Island Maid,* and the beautiful new side-
wheeler *Island Queen* were shuttling passengers to Coney Island.

Most of the packet steamers and excursion boats had a calliope.
They kept the valley filled with renditions of "Beautiful Ohio, Down
by the Ohio, Drifting and Dreaming, At Twilight Time," and "Drifting
Back to Dreamland."

It wasn't long until we reached Louisville, Ky. It was the site of
the Falls of the Ohio and the Louisville and Portland Canal. Dug
through sandstone rock by slave labor in the early 1800's the canal
was a bypass for boat traffic around the Falls. It was 339 miles from
our starting point at Point Pleasant.

"THE GATEWAY TO THE SOUTH," a signboard read as we
entered the 200-foot wide head of the canal and followed its two mile
course to the double locks at the lower end.

After we completed lockage we continued on our way to New
Albany, Indiana, on the opposite side of the river below the Falls.

The clear blue water of the Ohio was a fisherman's paradise. Dad
and the boys caught some of the biggest and sweetest tasting catfish
you ever ate. Men in johnboats tending trotlines and nets were a
common sight. Jug fishermen used 15 to 20 corked jugs rigged with
a bell and single line with baited hook set adrift in the river, while
they waited in johnboats for the fish to bite and catch themselves.

On Sundays the Ohio was the scene of baptizings up and down
its banks. All of us would gather on deck and watch as the preacher
led his flock down to the river singing "Shall We Gather at the River."
All became quiet as the preacher prayed. Then using a long stick to
test his footing, he waded waist deep in the river. One by one he
baptized them "In the name of the Father, and of the Son, and of the
Holy Spirit."

People living along the rivers at that time were God fearing, like
us. Though a few religious fanatics thought all show people were
sinners and wouldn't patronize us, especially in the Bible Belt, most
of our audiences were made up of fine church-going people.

I remember hearing mother sing a special song, "I'm Saving Up
Coupons To Get One Of Those, Thousands and Thousands, The Lord
Only Knows," meaning she was going to have another baby.

Then she became very ill with a high fever. The nearest doctor
was at Owensboro, Kentucky. Finding a phone at the General Store,
at Enterprise, Ind., Dad called him to the boat. As soon as he pulled

up to the landing in his Model T Ford, Dad rushed him upstairs to our quarters. There he found mother suffering from acute peritonitis. She had to be taken to the hospital for treatment. The doctor offered to take her there in his car. Dad carried her off the boat to the car and got in the back seat with her. Then, with us watching and waving goodbye to her, they drove away.

As we continued to meet our engagements Mother remained on the critical list in the City Hospital in Owensboro. On the third day when Dad returned from visiting her, he told us she was feeling better, and would be able to come back home in a few days.

The following morning, May 19, we headed up the remote Green River. Dad said, "I never felt so good knowing your mother is going to be all right. I never saw the Green River look so pretty. Even the birds' singing sounds prettier than I have ever heard it. It was so peaceful this morning alone in the pilothouse."

As we pulled into the landing at Curdsville, Ky., a man shouted up to Dad, "Captain Reynolds, I have an emergency message for you from Owensboro. You are wanted at the hospital right away. Your wife has taken a turn for the worse and is not expected to live!"

He tore down from the pilothouse, and before the boat touched ground, leaped off and ran up the hill. Mr. Thompson, who owned the general store and livery, was waiting with a horse and buggy. Off they went, cross country to the hospital.

The day dragged by without any word from Dad. The show went on as scheduled. A large crowd was watching the performance, and Margaret and I were with Aunt Ida in the ticket office counting receipts, when Dad walked in and told us the tragic news that Mother had died.

Samuel Lippencott came on stage and stopped the show long enough to tell the audience, "Ladies and gentlemen, we have just received word that Captain Reynold's lovely 34 year old wife, Margaret, the mother of his five children, passed away in the Owensboro Hospital where she had been taken ill four days ago. Following a moment of silence, in remembrance of her, the show will continue in its entirety." Since the show was already in progress, the old adage, "The show must go on," applied.

Years later, Dad told me that while he held Mother in his arms for the last time she said, "Watch over Catherine, Tom. Tie her to the bedpost if you have to while you're moving the boats so she won't fall in the river and drown."

Next morning we were taken by limousine to the funeral home in Owensboro. Phonograph music was playing. There was a light blue casket with a blanket of red roses and gold ribbon inscribed BELOVED WIFE AND MOTHER. It was heartbreaking. I drew back, hiding my face in fear when Dad told me to look at Mother. Then

Josephine Lippencott took me in her arms and coaxed me saying, "Catherine, look at the pretty blue dress your mother has on. She is going to heaven, a happier place, and though you won't see her, she will be up in the clouds watching over you."

After we left the funeral home her body was shipped by rail to my widowed grandmother, Sarrah McGlone, for final memorial services and burial in Greenlawn Cemetery at Portsmouth, Ohio.

Back on the boat Dad told us kids, "Your mother is gone now. We're going to have to pull together, help each other, and learn how to get along without her. Marion, Hazel, Tommy, I want you to help keep an eye on Margaret and Catherine. Make sure they're not sitting by the fence with their feet sticking through the railing when we go into the locks. Make sure they don't go downstairs when the boats are moving. I don't want to hear any fighting, or squabbling going on between you. Do your jobs. Stay out of trouble and come to me if you have a problem and we'll work it out."

With the patience of Job, he never raised his voice to us in anger. With the gentle understanding of losing his own mother at an early age, he became both father and mother to us. Though he had to rely on Aunt Ida to look after Margaret and me when he moved the boats, he took care of us the rest of the time.

Years later he said, "Catherine, you were my biggest problem, far more trouble to look after than Margaret, because you were crippled. I couldn't take my eyes off you for fear that you'd end up in the river drowned." Mother's last words haunted him.

Soon he began teaching me how to swim off the lower side deck of the *Atta Boy*. He tied a rope around me. I could splash up a storm dog-paddling with my hands, and I could kick a little with my right leg and foot. The left one hung limp in the water, weighing me down. I couldn't move it against he pressure of the water, but Dad kept encouraging me, and my legs grew stronger.

Two or three times a day he put me in the river and walked a complete circle around the showboat and towboat, across the paddle wheel, with me paddling along beside him. I stayed in the water until my lips turned blue and my skin wrinkled up like a dried prune. He stayed there beside me.

Before long he was letting slack in the line. I was learning to swim in spite of my handicap, and in time my leg muscles would strengthen so I would be able to walk on my own again . . . thanks to Dad and the beautiful river at our doorstep.

Mrs. Lippencott began to teach me the three R's, giving me a head start in my school work, hoping that someday I'd be able to walk to school with the other kids. My spelling lessons included the names of the showboats.

Sometimes, when Aunt Ida was busy, Uncle Tegie took us to the pilothouse. While Dad piloted the boat with his foot, he entertained us with stories about the places and people in the towns along the river.

The Green River, named for its color, flows in a northwesterly direction approximately 370 miles and empties into the Ohio River eight miles above Evansville, Indiana. There were no manufacturing plants or large cities along the river, only small country towns and villages shut off from the outside world except for the river. They were dependent on the Evansville and Bowling Green packet boats for exchange, the one deck Mailboat for communication, and the show-boats for their entertainment.

Most of the towns had a manual or motor operated ferry. Sometimes the towns were so isolated by poor roads that Marion and Tommy couldn't go ahead of the boat to post our bills. So our posters, along with free passes to the show, were sent by the small Mailboat to the postmaster who put them up for us.

At one whistle stop we were hemmed in along both sides of the river by a deep forest. Except for the wagon road leading down to the river there was no sign of anyone living there. The hill country was full of farm families who heard the calliope music and would come to the show that evening after their work was done. We had the day all to ourselves. We camped out in the wilderness, had a wonderful time swimming, fishing, hiking, sleeping and enjoying the beautiful scenery.

At supper, Frank Barton delighted in telling us this story, "I walked a couple of miles inland along the road looking for a town and all I saw was a farmhouse with an old-timer sitting on the front porch with his jug of corn liquor and hound dog. 'Good afternoon!' I called to him.

"He looked me over from head to toe and then said, 'How-dy, young feller. You must be one of them actors off the showboat.'

"Yes, sir, I am. Could you direct me to the town?" I asked.

"'Yur lookin' at hit, Sonny,' he said"

No one came down to the river to see the showboat during the early part of the day, or to hear the six-thirty playing of the calliope. But, with its second playing, they came by the wagon loads, on horseback and by foot. Marion was kept busy ferrying people across the river in our sixteen-passenger skiff. By show time a good paying crowd was gathered on board.

All was quiet on the river again after the show let out. Quiet, that is, until the bullfrogs came out and set up their mating chorus along the riverbanks. Then, while the rest of the crew slept, Dad and the boys slipped out in the skiff with flashlights and gunny sacks to catch frogs for supper.

Next morning there was a big cage setting on deck outside our quarters. It was full of frogs that were trying to escape. So, feeling sorry for them, I opened the door and let them out. Splash! They hit the water one after the other. Nothing was said about it, but the following morning the cage was gone. Dad had moved it to the engine room, and we ended up having fried frog legs on the menu as planned.

The farther we traveled the more narrow the Green River became, and dangerous to navigate. Soon we were running so close to the riverbanks on each side we could reach out and touch the tree branches. There was no room to pass another boat. There was barely room for us to squeeze through. We were frequently stopped by sharp curves blocking passage. We had to back and fill several times before making it around them. Finally the boats had to be uncoupled and swung clockwise around them with a tow rope before we could continue on our way.

From Curdsville we stopped at all the little towns between Delaware and Brownsville, 149 miles inland, on Green River.

One morning I was in the pilothouse with Dad when we headed on our last jump upriver. Frank Barton and the Great Ellwood were also there talking and taking in the sights as we maneuvered along the narrow crooked stream. We were stopped by a low lying cliff that blocked our passage. It looked like a black cloud hanging over the side of the river in front of us. Dad sized it up from top to bottom and said, "Take Catherine and go below deck. I'm going to ram her through."

Then the boat began backing up, getting ready for the run. With the engine picking up momentum he nosed the showboat toward the cliff. It hit the pilothouse and tore off the roof., but we kept on going to Mammoth Cave, Kentucky. The *Majestic* was the only showboat, and the largest craft ever to venture that far up the Green River.

We arrived at Mammoth Cave on June 15, 1925. It was still in its exploratory stage and relatively unknown to the outside world. The explorer, Floyd Collins, in February 1925, had become lost in the cavern while searching for a new entrance to Crystal Cave.

Daily newspaper reports, radio broadcasts and newsreels had reported rescue efforts and it was like a three-ring circus. Visitors from all over the country flocked to the area to see the site where he lost his life.

The boat landing was in a beautiful setting of forested hills and rugged cliffs with cave openings. Ganter Cave was on the right side of the landing path at the top of the hill. From where we sat on deck we could look into the cave entrance, which was lighted with gas lamps, and watch the people going in and out of it. The pathway leading down to the boat was lined with vegetation and wildflowers.

There were no houses in sight, or other boats on that part of the river besides us.

Local residents had concession stands set up near the cave entrance selling souvenirs to the visitors. As soon as we pulled into the landing, one of them moved his stand near the foot of the gangplank and sold his wares to visitors coming down to the boat. His number one seller was what he alleged to be chips off the boulder that pinned Floyd Collins to his death in Crystal Cave. Stories of the unusual things they saw in the cave was the main topic at the supper table. They enjoyed telling about the glass bottom boat ride they took on Echo River, where fish with no eyes were seen swimming 360 feet below the earth's surface.

Due to the interest shown by the visitors to the boat we played a double engagement there. Instead of the regular dramatic presentation, we put on a musical revue plus chorus girls in line singing and dancing to "Five Foot Two, Ain't She Sweet, The Charleston," and "The Black Bottom," with Dixieland accompaniment. It was in keeping with the Roaring Twenties Flapper Girl look and the Dance Follies craze that was sweeping the country. The audience loved it.

Next morning we began backing our way downriver pulling the showboat from behind with the *Atta Boy* instead of pushing her. It was time consuming and dangerous. Backing into the tiny lock chambers and making double lockage without going over the dam was tricky. We continued in that manner over a hundred miles before the river was wide enough to turn the *Majestic* around and resume her normal head first position. Finally, with Curdsville and Spottsville the last stops, we continued onto the Ohio River again.

We stopped at Henderson, Kentucky, were auctioneers could be heard selling tobacco in the warehouse at the top of the hill. At Elizabethtown, Illinois, we got stuck on a sandbar lying hidden beneath the surface of the water, in the middle of the river, and had to be pulled off by a U. S. Government boat.

We showed at Smithland, Ky., at the mouth of the Cumberland River; Paducah, Ky., at the mouth of the Tennessee River; and Cairo, Illinois, at the junction of the Mississippi River, 981 miles from Pittsburgh.

Then we began working our way back up the Ohio. The temperature was over 100 degrees every day. There wasn't a breath of air. Dad sprayed the roof deck of the showboat with river water to help cool the theatre every evening before the show. The only way we could beat the heat was to get into the river.

Uncle Tegie, Marion, Hazel, Tommy and the actors played a daring game called, "Catch the Boat." A rope with a large knot at the end was hung from the stern of the skiff. Then they took turns diving off the corner bow of the showboat into the river and caught the rope before it passed by. It was tricky, as they could miss the rope and the boat. Sure enough, one morning the Great Ellwood missed. Dad just happened to glance out the pilothouse window and saw his head bobbing up and down in our wake. Sounding the emergency whistle, he stopped the boat long enough for Marion to pick him up in the skiff. Though shaken, he was laughing and ready to do it again as soon as he got his wind back. After that a guard was posted to make sure no one else got left behind.

There was also a rope swing on the lower back deck of the showboat to dive from at the landings. It could only be used when that side of the boat was facing the river. With Dad the ringleader, we all had fun playing on it. Even two year old Margaret, who learned to swim before she could walk, took turns swinging out over the river to where Dad waited for us to drop into his arms.

Dad told me not to go down the stairs or near the rope when he wasn't there to look after me. Of course, one day I did, and nearly killed myself.

We were lying below the Ohio Falls at New Albany, Indiana. The riverbank was covered with soft, gooey mud. We couldn't swim off the rope that day because it was facing the riverbank, but Hazel and Tommy were having a wonderful time swinging out over the riverbank and back.

At the sound of their voices, I went midway the stairs and sat there watching them for awhile. "Let me have a turn," I pleaded.

"No, Caty, you're not allowed," Tommy reminded me.

So I waited until they left and slipped down the stairs and across the deck where they had left the rope hanging off the wall hook. Glancing around, I didn't see Dad or anyone else. So, I took hold of the rope and gave myself a shove off the deck with my good leg. For a blissful moment I glided through the air. Then my hands began slipping off the rope and I fell into the mud head first. It was like diving into the water. It just swallowed me up. Holding my breath, I desperately tried to extricate myself but the more I tried the more deeply embedded in the mire I became. I gasped for air, swallowed mud, and felt faint.

Luckily, Dad came out of the engine room and say my feet sticking up through the mud. One look and he knew it was me. Hopping in the skiff he quickly came to my rescue. He didn't scold me or spank me for not minding. But, later he told me, "Catherine, I was so aggravated with you for a second I had a good notion of leaving you there in the mud, but thought better of it."

Along one section of the river we saw a lot of Klan action. We saw the Klansmen marching with torches along the river roads near the boat and burning crosses on the hill tops while the show was going on. One night we blacked out because of racial unrest. The people were afraid to leave their homes. Another time there was a mob lynching taking place in the town square as we pulled into the landing with calliope playing.

A little black youth at the landing told Dad, "They's hangin' a Nig'r fo' rapin' a white woman."

Uncle Tegie and Frank Barton went uptown and witnessed the hanging, confirming the boy's story. The show went on as scheduled that night, but the actors were careful of what they said and did. One of the showboats did run into some Klan opposition because of the dialog used in their play, *"The American Council."*

One day we played a double engagement at a town with the Barnum and Bailey Circus. So, we all went to see the matinee performance under the big top. We also went to the Cincinnati Zoo when the boat played nearby.

The saddest time was when Dad took us to see Mother's grave at Portsmouth, Ohio. Having kept his grief bottled up inside, he broke down at the sight of her headstone and stark mound of dirt. He told us, "I did not realize how much I loved your mother, or how much she meant to me until she died. She was a wonderful woman. I hope all of you girls grow up to be like her." I remember looking up in the clouds for a glimpse of Mother's face.

At Cattlettsburg, Kentucky we went up the Big Sandy River. Only small craft with light drafts could navigate it. The *Majestic* was the only showboat her size to venture up the Sandy, and her calliope the only one heard in the area. Playing to good business we made stops along the way to the head of navigation at Louisa Fork, Ky., 45 miles above the mouth. It was like a short sight-seeing trip along a seldom traveled lane off the main highway. It was our only trip up the Big Sandy.

I was in the Pilothouse with Dad the morning we passed the *Water Queen* Showboat lying at New Martinsville, W. Va. She was being dolled up with banners and bunting. Captain and Josie Hyatt had leased the showboat to the Famous Players - Lasky Film Corporation for the filming of Gloria Swanson's latest silent moving picture, *"Stage Struck."* The boat's name was temporarily changed to the *Gloria Swanson.*

One hundred and seventeen people were on board for the making of the movie, including Miss Swanson. All the Hyatt's regular cast of showboat players were extras in the film.

Josie Hyatt told us, "Miss Swanson was awfully nice. She was common as she could be. She took off her shoes and stockings and went barefoot on the boat and in swimming during her leisure time like the rest of us. Every morning there would be a large crowd of people standing on he riverbank waiting to get a look at her and the other movie people. By the time they finished making the movie we were all starry-eyed from the bright lights and the glamour of having them on board. It sure was exciting!"

In September we headed up the Kanawha River for a tour of the mining and industrial towns. All went well until we came to the rapids at Redhouse Chute. Several times Dad tried nosing the showboat above it, but bogged down near the head and was helplessly swept back by the swift water. There wasn't enough engine power to make it. So, everyone who could pull their own weight, Aunt Ida, the actors and actresses, Hazel and Tommy lined up along the shore with a tow rope. Then, with Marion in the engine room goosing the engine, and Uncle Tegie on the front of the showboat tending the line, and those on the riverbank pulling and straining, we slowly inched our way up through the rapids to the ferry landing at Winfield, W. Va., above the chute.

We played all the towns on both sides of the river. At Boncar, 95 miles above the mouth of the Kanawha, we were hemmed in by towering mountains. We could only see the sun when it was straight overhead at high noon.

The forest was adorned with a coat of fall colors and there was a chill in the air. The 32-week tour was brought to a close in mid-October and we returned to the Kingtown Landing, at Point Pleasant, W. Va. for another winter . . . this one without Mother.

Chapter 7
The Captain and His Kids

That winter Dad could have won the "Mother of the Year" award. He did everything Mother would have done had she been there. He did the laundry on the board, ironed and mended clothes, wiped runny noses, bandaged my knees every time I fell down, and nursed Margaret and me through the measles and whooping cough. He also cooked three meals a day from scratch.

Wearing one of Mother's wraparound aprons and his shirtsleeves rolled up to his elbows, he'd call us to the table with a cherry, "Come and get it while it's hot." For breakfast he fried all the pancakes we could eat smothered with maple syrup and margarine. Then after the kids left for school, he put an iron pot of pinto beans, seasoned with fatback and garlic, on he stove to cook while he did the housework. At noon he baked a pan of cornbread and had it and the beans on the table waiting when they came in on their lunch break.

For supper he either had vegetable soup, beef stew, spaghetti with meatballs, meat and potato meals, or mush and milk. He also baked bread, cakes, cookies or berry pies. He was a good cook, having learned from necessity as a young man. Mother's old recipe files came in handy when he needed help.

Instead of my summer swimming therapy Dad took me to Dr. Roy Eshenar every Saturday for chiropractic treatments. His office was on the second floor of the Spencer Hotel. The treatments were very painful. To help compensate for it, he took me to see the movie playing at the Alpine or Lyric Theatre afterwards. Having that to look forward to, I didn't mind going to the doctor nearly as much.

One day we went through the Mansion House at Tu-Endi-Wei Park and saw the collection of colonial furniture, Indian artifacts and memorabilia from "The Battle of Point Pleasant" stored there. He also showed me the location of the log cabin, where he was born, just north of the park. He pointed out the double story block building that was The Last Chance Saloon, now Neace's Grocery Store, where we bought most of our groceries.

He held my hand as we made the mile walk into town and back. I loved every minute of it. I didn't wear leg braces then. Dad thought they were more of a hindrance than a help. His theory was the more I exercised my leg muscles, the quicker I would overcome my handicap. In my case he was right.

Dad was a wonderful storyteller. In the evening we kids and our cousins loved to sit on the floor in front of him in his rocking chair and listen to him tell the stories in episodes. Like the old silent movies and with such realism it was like being there. He'd build them up to an exciting scene, like a gang of wild Indians chasing Cowboy Pete to the edge of a high cliff, and then say, "The story is continued until tomorrow night."

He guided us with a firm, but loving hand. Though the older kids were taught to defend themselves against bullies, we weren't allowed to bicker and fight among ourselves. When a squabble broke out, his softly spoken, "That'll be enough of that," usually stopped it. If the warning went unheeded, he took the troublemakers one at a time by the arm and gave them a resounding slap on the seat of their breeches. If that wasn't enough to restore order, or it was a serious offense, he got the razor strap off the wall hook and let it do the talking for him. He kept us living peacefully together in the close confines of our winter quarters.

He wasn't being abusive. It was his way of teaching respect for him, the authority figure, and for each other's rights. Though I never got any spankings, I am grateful for this early training. If I did anything wrong, all he had to do was draw his frown down, give me a disappointed look, and I'd straighten right up.

Knowing Mother would have wanted us to continue in our Christian training, he took Margaret and me as far as the front door for Sunday School, and came and got us when it was over. We also attended services with Aunt Fan and our cousins.

Christmas Eve the showboat kids helped put on the program at church. While we were gone Dad set up the candlelit tree in the front room and got everything ready for a visit from Santa. There was one special gift for each of us placed under the tree, plus candy, fruit, nuts and good things to eat.

The winter slipped by, and with the annual ice run safely behind us, it was time to head on our summer tour again.

With all new faces in the cast, except the family actors, we opened the show at Point Pleasant on April 3, 1926. *"The Girl in the Case,"* a mystery drama, plus five specialties, five chorus girls, and orchestra was presented. Then, with rain and stormy weather following us, we headed downbound on the Ohio.

A *Billboard* review said, "THE *MAJESTIC* SHOW-BOAT, owned and operated by Nicol and Reynolds, was the first of the fleet which brings entertainment to the people who live in the river towns to visit Constance, Kentucky, opposite Riverside, a suburb of Cincinnati. The boat arrived early Monday morning, April 26, after coming down the river from a point below Chilo.

Because of the heavy rains during the few days preceding the boat's visit the roads in the vicinity were quite muddy, and this, with the cold weather, held the attendance down to about 250. However, tho small in number, the audience appreciated the fine performance.

Starting at eight o'clock, a 15 minute overture was given by the three piece orchestra. Then began an interesting presentation of Robert Sherman's *"The Girl in the Case."* The mystery end of the play was carried through to perfection.

The play itself has all the elements that make a good one . . . action, romance, and love . . . and the small company on the *Majestic* took advantage of every opportunity offered it to put the play across.

Between acts, vaudeville specialties were given by various members of the company and Hazel Reynolds. The setting was adequate, though small.

In the company are Earl Hunter, producer; Edith Hunter, Jack Brady, Gladys Hyde, Estelle Woods, Al Court, Eddie Jackson, Edith Jackson and Tom Reynolds. Tom Reynolds also handles the stage, while Tegie Nicol, manager, is on the door, and Mrs. Nicol is at the ticket office.

Both before and after the performance a visit was made to various members of the company in their staterooms on the boat. All seemed happy and contented and are looking forward to a good season. Although the boat has been out since the third of April, business has been rather poor due to bad weather. At Chilo, Ohio, no performance was given because of the heavy rain.

The *Majestic* will continue down the river, playing practically all the river towns, and will not head back upstream again until the middle of the season."

The *America* was the second showboat of the season to visit Constance, where they too played to a small crowd due to bad weather. Their three piece orchestra played a 30 minute overture before the curtain went up on the first act of the play *"Traffic in Souls."* Vaudeville specialties by each member of the cast were given between acts. Here again, Uncle Bill had let some of his actors go, and was short of cast until new ones arrived. But the bill was highly pleasing to the audience.

The cast included Uncle Bill, who handled one of the leading roles; Jack Gerand, Billie Gerand, who was also the piano and calliope player; Harry Van, Mrs. Van; Martin Burke, leads; Grandpa, Aunt Fan, and Ida Mae Reynolds. *"The Trial of Mary"* was their alternate bill.

Dad bought a shiny new Model T Ford. We transported it from town to town on the head of the showboat. It was used for billing. He also took us kids and anyone else that could squeeze into the car on joy rides through the countryside. It opened up a whole new world to me, a world away from the river. Up and down we went over rough roads and along the wagon trails through creek beds. The deer and other wildlife scurried out of our way. Dropping into deep ruts we had to pile out of the car and wait until Dad worked it back onto the road. It was a wonderful feeling coming back through town and seeing our boats and the river again.

Getting the car off the boat and back on it again without losing it in the river was like watching a three-ring circus. The gangplank, was only wide enough to run one side of the car on it, so an extension was placed next to it.

The front end of the car was manually lifted off the deck onto the planks and the wheels lined up. Then with Marion at the wheel, holding it steady, and Uncle Tegie in front of the car holding and guiding it down the planks, and Dad pushing and holding from behind, and all of us on deck watching and laughing, they rolled it lopsided down the wobbling planks off the boat onto the bank. It was tricky. Sometimes Uncle Tegie had to hop in the water to keep the car from falling off. We found that hilarious!

Usually there was a dirt ferry road or paved wharf where the car could be run up the hill. But in unimproved locations the car had to be pulled by block and tackle up the embankment. Occasionally it was impossible to move it off the boat.

Coming to the Kentucky River junction, 280 miles from Point Pleasant, we entered its narrow mouth for a brief tour. Carrollton, Kentucky was our first stop.

Every now and then we saw a gasboat with some coal or oil barges go by. We also shared some of the landings with a small packet boat.

Playing to good business, we continued making stops at Locust Grove, Marshall Bottom, Lockport, Leestown, and Frankfort, Kentucky, the state capitol, for a double engagement.

"Freckles" was the alternate bill. There were song and dance numbers by the chorus and vaudeville specialties.

Marion, my 15 year old brother, starred in the title role of Freckles.

Back on the Ohio we continued south to the Green River junction. There we made a round trip tour of the towns to Brownsville, 17½ miles below Mammoth Cave, and back. We continued south to the Cumberland River junction at Smithland, Ky., for a full house. Then we began our long trip back up the Ohio River playing towns en route to the Kanawha River.

By this time I had mastered swimming in spite of my handicap, and had more freedom of movement in the water than out. Instead of the rope tied around me for security Dad rowed alongside me in the skiff when I swam.

I could be swimming along, and suddenly double up with leg cramp. Dropping the oars, he'd reach out and catch me before I sank. Because of that, I wasn't allowed in the water unless he was there to keep an eye on me. But, being the mischievous brat that I was, I began slipping downstairs and just "accidently" falling overboard with my clothes on.

I got away with it several times and I was swimming around having a wonderful time when Dad appeared on deck above me.

"Catherine, what are you doing in the river?" he asked.

"I fell in," I innocently replied.

Though I'm sure he knew I was lying, he sat down on the checkpost and told me, "Go ahead and swim," and he stayed there watching until I got tired. "Now, let me see you go on the riverbank and walk up the gangplank onto the boat by yourself."

Struggling to walk through the water was the most difficult part, and it took a while to walk the length of the showboat along the bank, but I finally made it. He could see how much stronger my legs had become.

After that, with his supervision I swam and played in the river with Hazel, Tommy and Margaret. Children from the town came down to the boat and swam with us. Some of them became long lasting friends.

October 15th we wound up the season playing along the Kanawha River to the Falls, and back to Kingtown for the winter.

The *America* was also tied up there for the winter, as well as several other showboats. All reported doing well that season in spite of the rain and swift water.

That fall Dad enrolled me in the first grade at Central School, where he had attended as a boy. I had improved enough to walk the half mile to school and back with the older kids. Miss Stanforth was my teacher. Thanks to Mrs. Lippencott's tutoring I had no trouble keeping up with the class. I couldn't make it home for dinner and back to school in time for afternoon classes, so Dad packed a bag lunch and gave me a nickle for milk. I couldn't participate in some of the physical games my classmates played, but they were kind and included me in the games I could play.

January 22, 1927, General John McCausland, Confederate States of America, died at the age of 91 at his home near South Side, West Virginia. Due to flooding, the roads were under water and the family was unable to transport his body to the burial site. They were also unable to find a boat and pilot who would do the job until they asked Dad. Point Pleasant was a Union town, and memories and feelings still ran deep concerning the Civil War and General McCausland.

With me riding in the pilothouse and Grandpa tending the lines, we traveled up the rain swollen Kanawha to the McCausland Landing.

There the Confederate flag draped coffin was brought on board and placed on supports in front of the pilothouse, followed by the family of mourners all dressed in black. The flag was removed from the coffin and placed on the *Atta Boy's* jackstaff in tribute to the General.

Then, with the Confederate flag flying proudly in the wind, we moved past the "Point" and continued downstream on the Ohio where the General's body was removed and taken to the cemetery by horse and wagon. General McCausland's Confederate flag was the last to be flown aboard a riverboat on the Kanawha River, and it was flown aboard the *Atta Boy.*

In gratitude to Dad for his kindness and unbiased service, John McCausland, Jr. gave him exclusive hunting rights on their large estate for as long as he lived. It was a special honor, since no one was allowed to step foot on their land without permission. Dad hunted there for many years.

In March the Menke Brother's *Goldenrod Showboat* left with a company of Universal Studio picture people on board. They were filming Edna Ferber's fictional novel, *"Showboat."* The movie would boost the image and popularity of old-time showboats.

April 3, 1927 we opened at Leon, West Virginia with *"Clouds and Sunshine,"* vaudeville specialties and the girls' chorus. The roster included Al Tint, heavy; Mabel Ford, ingenue; Walter Johnson, general business; Marea Mack, characters; Earl Hunter, director and characters; Edith Hunter, leads, piano and calliope; Joe Lions, general business; Hazel Reynolds, specialties and parts; Tom Reynolds, parts and trap drummer for the orchestra.

"The Horseradish King" was the opening bill aboard the *America* and kept the patrons in an uproar from beginning to end.

The cast included Uncle Bill, comedian; Jack Gerand, heavies and specialties; Billie Gerand, heavies and specialties, piano and calliope; Jean Colin, juvenile; Helen King, dancer; Ida Mae Reynolds, dancer; Aunt Fan, tickets and candy; Grandpa, tickets and John Davis, bill poster.

"Hush Money" was their alternate bill.

In May, shortly after our arrival at Portland, Ohio, Dad asked me, "Do you like Garnett Neal?"

"Yes," I said.

"Do you like her enough to have her come and live with us, and be your stepmother?"

"Yes," I replied without hesitation.

Garnett was the pretty young woman who lived in the double house on he waterfront at Kingtown. I passed by there going and coming from school every day. When I saw her I always stopped and talked with her for awhile. Apparently Dad did too.

One day he brought her down to the boat and showed her around. He also took her to the opening night performance aboard the *New Sensation,* which opened its season at Point Pleasant, after spending the winter there.

So, with Aunt Ida and Uncle Tegie's blessings, he left on the train to Point Pleasant and brought her back to the boat with him as his blushing bride.

That evening after the show, when he and Garnett came upstairs for the night, we all sneaked on deck outside our quarters until their light went out. Then like an army invasion, we began yelling, blowing whistles, horns, bells, beating on drums, pans, setting off firecrackers, and making it thunder and lightning with stage props. That brought them laughing and giggling to the door. We sang "For He's a Jolly Good Fellow." Then we all gathered in the dining room aboard the *Atta Boy* for homemade ice cream and cake.

Garnett fit right in with our way of life on the river. She loved children and was a wonderful stepmother and companion to us. A born housekeeper and cook, she went to work helping Aunt Ida and Hazel in the kitchen, and was ticket taker for the show. Being a pretty good dancer, she joined the girls' chorus, bringing the number to six, including Hazel.

With Earl Hunter and Uncle Tegie coaching her in the part, Garnett also played the role of Rita, a native girl in the South Sea Island drama, *"Jealousy."* In one scene she performed the hula with strumming guitars and drum beats in the background.

Garnett smoked cigarettes. Dad didn't like to see her do it and told her, "I'd much rather see you smoke a corn cob pipe instead of puffing on one of those things." So she bought a pipe and bag of tobacco, but only smoked it when he was with her. When he wasn't, she smoked her cigarettes, and I was her lookout, telling her when Dad was coming.

1927 was another prosperous season for all the showboats, including Doc Bart's *Ark* Showboat. It opened the season with a production of *"Uncle Tom's Cabin"* with 28 people in the cast, six of whom were black. He later traded the company of actors for a trained animal show, featuring lions and elephants.

With the *America* playing towns a week or so behind us, we made follow-up tours of the Muskingum, Upper Ohio and Monongahela Rivers, then closed the show in October and tied up at Clyde's Landing at Glenwood, Pa., for the winter. Soon the America joined us and we laid nose to nose at the landing.

Dad went back to work doing commercial towing with the *Atta Boy* while Garnett took on the job of cooking and looking after us. Instead of doing the laundry on the washboard, she bought a Maytag washing machine with a gasoline motor.

In the evening after school Grandpa helped Ida Mae, Hazel and the boys build a playground on the riverbank, at the top of the hill. Using old railroad ties found along the bank they built a merry-go-round, teeter totter, a one room cabin we called the "Showboat Kid's Playhouse," and hung a tree swing.

We played outside until winter dumped tons of snow and ice, then played house inside the cabin. Ida Mae and Hazel had furnished it with curtains, furniture, pots and pans, food stuff, oil lamp, and a one lid coal stove. The cabin also had a front porch. We spent many happy hours there playing house, popping corn, cooking potato and onion soup, and tried to beat each other at checkers and dominoes.

Hoboes traveling to and fro on trains moving past the boats were a common sight. Occasionally one would come on board and knock on our door asking for food. Garmett always fixed them sandwiches, hot coffee and cake or pie. They never offered to harm us in any way, and no one left empty-handed.

One morning we awoke to find smoke rising from the playhouse smokestack. Some hoboes saw how inviting it was while passing by on the train, got off and moved in. It was bound to happen. When Dad told them it belonged to us kids, they left riding the rails just like they came.

Garnett was afraid of their coming to our door at night while we were asleep or when Dad was away at his job. One night we saw a flashing light and someone outside our window, we hid under the covers until daylight. It was cousin Ida Mae, who loved to tease, playing a trick on us.

The eight older showboat kids liked to gather in the auditorium of the showboats and put on a show. With Ida Mae and Hazel trying to keep the boys in line, and me in the pit trying to play the piano, they took turns mimicking the comedy bits and skits we'd seen the actors do the previous summer. The boys, who had two left feet and couldn't carry a tune in a bucket, sang and danced in a chorus line with Hazel and Ida Mae. It was great fun and you could hear us laughing all over the boat.

I learned to perform a variety of acrobatic stunts in gym class at the Township Pebbles School in Glenwood. I could do everything my classmates could do except the back bend. My knee buckled as I leaned back, but I could flip forward, then drop to my knees and bend back with my feet touching the top of my head and roll over like a ball.

We attended the vaudeville show at the Harris Theatre in downtown Pittsburgh where a lady contortionist headed the bill. I couldn't take my eyes off her, concentrating on her every move. Back at the boat I told Dad, "I think I can do her act."

"Let's see if you can," he said. After watching me perform he took me to show Uncle Tegie. He and Aunt Ida watched me perform one stunt after another. "By golly, Tom, I think Catherine has something. With a little coaching we can use her in the show this summer."

"It's all right with me, if it is with Catherine. Would you like to do an act this summer?" he asked with a broad grin.

"Oh, yes, I will, I will!" I happily exclaimed, and spent much time after that in front of a mirror practicing my stunts.

The biggest event that took place in our lives that spring was the birth of my half sister, Ruth, aboard the *Majestic*. Dad's life was complete again with Garnett and the new baby in his arms. We were all happy as could be.

The closer it came to our opening, date the harder I worked. With Aunt Ida's supervision I cut out and sewed a black and white satin costume to wear in my act. After the actors arrived and rehearsals got underway, I practiced my act on stage. My two greatest admirers, Dad and Uncle Tegie, sat out front in the theatre encouraging me.

Earl and Edith Hunter, Al Court, and Gladys Hyde were back for another season. Ernie and Jeanie St. Clair, characters and dance team, and Billy and Alma Van, characters, made up the professional cast. The extras were Dad, Uncle Tegie, Hazel, Tommy, and me.

Chapter 8
My Stage and Calliope Debut

"Here comes the showboat! Here comes the showboat!" Edith Hunter played the calliope as we traveled up the Monongahela River, April 10, 1928, en route to Elrama, Pa. for our opening night performance.

The song "Here Comes the Showboat" was the adopted theme song and symbol of the traveling showboats that spring. It was being heard for the first time all up and down the river. "Here Comes the Showboat," was first introduced to the general public in the movie, Showboat, in the fall of 1927.

In addition to my appearance in the vaudeville lineup, I was given my first job out front as usherette that evening.

Edith Hunter, the "Ragtime Piano Gal," and Dad, the trap drummer, opened the show with "Maple Leaf Rag, Pineapple Rag," and the "Black and White Rag."

Then, playing to a full house, the curtain went up on the 4 act comedy drama, "The Gorilla." The gorilla was Al Court in a realistic gorilla costume. I sat back and watched the plot unfold until the end of the third act. Then went backstage with Aunt Ida to get ready for my act.

The dressing room was a beehive of activity with the actresses changing costumes and re-doing their makeup. They smiled and moved over to make room for me. Then I sat down in front of the dressing table spread with combs, brushes, and tubes of greasepaint. She went to work on me saying, "Now watch how I do this and you'll be able to put on your own makeup after awhile."

She covered my hairline with a towel and spread a layer of foundation makeup on my face and neck, rouged my cheeks, and put on royal blue eye shadow. Using a lighted candle, she melted a small container of black mascara over the flame and used it to line my lids and darken my eyebrows. She beaded my lashes, painted my lips and applied medium dark powder to keep me from looking like a ghost in front of the footlights.

Then she helped me into my costume and smoothed down my hair while the actresses watched and smiled their approval. "Don't forget to smile at the audience. Take bows and do your routine like you practiced it," she said.

"I will," I assured her, and went to the wings where I watched Earl Hunter performing his magic act.

"Catherine, are you scared?" Dad asked in a low whisper as he slipped up beside me.

"No," I said, not taking my eyes off the magician.

"There's nothing to be afraid of," he told me with a twinkle in his eyes. "When Earl gives your cue, go out there and show them what you can do."

We watched Earl make white doves and rabbits appear and disappear and turn water into wine. He took the bottle and shot glasses out into the audience to anyone who wanted to taste it for authenticity. Two men told the audience, "It's wine all right. It's the real thing, there is no doubt about it."

Back on stage Earl tapped the lower part of the bottle with a mallet until it separated, and out ran three white mice.

"Oh, my Lord! I think I'm going to be sick!" The wine taster on the front row said.

"I think I'm going to die!" moaned the other taster, causing fits of laughter and applause.

After his act's completion, Earl, who was also the master of ceremonies, bounced back on stage and said, "Ladies and gentlemen! Captain Reynolds' daughter, Catherine, is coming on stage next to entertain you. At the age of three, Catherine was stricken with infantile paralysis which left her paralyzed below the waist. But with exercises, swimming, and determination to overcome her affliction, Catherine attends school and can do most anything she wants to. If anyone in the audience is handicapped in any way, we sincerely hope her appearance in the show will be an encouragement to you . . . And now, it is with great pleasure, and pride, that I give you The Little Girl Contortionist Who Overcame Infantile Paralysis . . . Miss Catherine Reynolds! . . . Let's welcome her with a big hand."

The curtain rose, spotlighting me in center stage doing the splits, posing with head tilted and arms raised above my head framing my face. I held the position smiling at the sea of faces in the crowd until all was quiet.

Then I went into my act, twisting, bending and balancing my body in various positions, doing the standing splits, cartwheels, forward flips, and dropping to my knees and rolling across the stage like a ball with my feet touching the back of my head. For my last stunt I placed two chairs side by side in center stage. Then I climbed on them, with one foot on each chair, and slowly spread the chairs apart until I was suspended in the splits. I smiled, struck up a pose, and held it until the curtain fell.

Applause roared over the theatre without let up. I had stopped the show. The applause was music to my ears. What a wonderful feeling.

"They love you," Earl told me. "Go back and take a bow."

I stepped out in front of the street drop smiling and said, "Thank you. Thank you." Then flipped over and dropped to the floor in the splits, turned a couple of handsprings, touched the back of my head with my foot, and went offstage to more applause.

The family and actors, who had been watching from the wings, nearly smothered me with hugs and compliments. The proud look and seldom spoken words of praise, "Catherine, you did fine," from Dad, was the most pleasing.

Then Ernie and Jeanie St. Clair performed an adagio dance; Billy and Alma Van, a comedy bit, singing and dancing and Hazel Reynolds, a cornet solo.

I returned on stage with the rest of the cast for the grand finale. We sang "Here Comes the Showboat." Then Hazel and I joined Garnett out front bidding the patrons goodnight and thanking them for their compliments about my act and the show. Dad and Uncle Tegie shook hands and bid them farewell as they went up the hill.

I performed nightly in the show, and repeated my acrobatic act on our return engagements. *"Her Secret Lover,"* a three act comedy drama, plus five acts of vaudeville, and the Girl's Chorus was the alternate bill.

For my work out front and in the show I was given $3 a week in quarters. At first I put every quarter I made into slot machines at ice cream parlors, thinking I might win the jackpot, but lost it all. One day Garnett dropped one quarter in a machine and won! Holding up her skirt to catch the money that poured out like a river. She laughed and laughed. That did it! No more gambling for me. After that I saved most of my money and watched it grow in my school bank account.

I also made a little extra money catching fish worms. Jeanie St. Clair gave me a dime for a tin can full of worms. She put them in the hot sun on the roof deck of the *Atta Boy* and used their melted oil to make her limbs and joints limber for her adagio dance.

I was frequently asked to meet a handicapped child who wanted to make my acquaintance. It was surprising to see how many girls and boys there were stricken by infantile paralysis. Accompanied by their relatives they came limping, on crutches, in wheelchairs, and in some instances, carried on board. Some were so severely handicapped they would never be any better. They were outgoing with me. We had a nice time laughing and talking. They loved being on the showboat and getting to know us all. They were fascinated with the showboat, my family, and the actors.

While we talked and enjoyed one another's company, Dad and the parents were nearby talking and exchanging their knowledge and experiences of being parents of a handicapped child. Dad knew the contact I had with these children was good for me as well as them. I gave them hope that they could get better, too.

Earl Hunter was a fine musician. He astounded the audience everywhere with his sleight of hand tricks. He sawed Edith in half and put her back together again, and suspended her in air.

His popularity increased when a lady in the audience asked if he could tell her where she had lost her diamond engagement ring. Of course he didn't know, but he told her to take the trap off the kitchen sink and look in it.

The following day, while we were showing at the next town, she came to show him the ring on her finger. She couldn't thank him enough. The news spread from town to town bringing people from near and far away to see him perform.

Down the Ohio and up the Muskingum River we went. The weather was stormy the day we stopped at Beverly, Ohio inside the Lock Canal. It was evening and Dad had steam popping in the boiler to play the calliope. Then there was a flash of lightning across the sky, followed by a loud earthshaking boom. It was close and nearly scared us out of our wits. We hurried on deck to see what had happened.

The lightning struck the boiler. Luckily, it was grounded. Hot steam was pouring out of the broken glass gauge, which had to be replaced immediately. Dad went to work on it and suffered burns to his face, neck and arms.

In September we made our first trip up the Allegheny River. Three hundred and twenty five miles long, it joins the Monongahela to form the Ohio River. The Allegheny looked very shallow, but wasn't.

Letting the voice of the calliope "Here Comes the Showboat," do our advertising, we wildcatted the towns as we came to them. Drawing good crowds to overflowing crowds every place we stopped, Verona, Oakmont, Tarentum, Freeport, Ford City, Manorville, and Kittanning, Pa., forty five miles above the mouth of the river. It was said that the *Majestic* was the only showboat to ever go that far up the Allegheny River.

We received word that Aunt Fan was seriously ill in Pittsburgh. Returning to the city wharf, we laid over without showing for several days to be with Uncle Bill's family. Aunt Fan died September 13, 1928. Her body was shipped to Portsmouth, Ohio for burial next to mother in Greenlawn Cemetery. Like mother, Aunt Fan also left five children, including Pauline, born October 30, 1925.

During the tour Marion and Tommy had a little money making project of their own. Using the showboat hull for a barge, they filled it with scrap iron and junk they found laying along the riverbanks and sold it to a dealer in Pittsburgh. They tried to give part of their money to Dad, but he wouldn't take it.

We finished the remainder of the season revisiting towns along the Monongahela River and returned to Glenwood for the winter.

April 15, 1929, we opened at Elrama, Pa., and continued upbound on the Monongahela River.

May 18, *Billboard* reported:

"*Majestic* Clicking With Fans - Annabelle Montgomery, who is this season producing the show and musical numbers on the *Majestic* Showboat, writes in to tell us that the boat has been showing to good business since opening its season and that the crowds all along the line have been voicing their approval of the programs offered.

The *Majestic* is this season offering its patrons "*Kitty's Birthday, Handcuffs and Airplane,*" together with a good line of bits, musicals and seven good vaudeville acts. The *Majestic's* personnel include Victor LaZelle and Doc Houston, comics; Tom Nicol, characters; Charles Montgomery, piano and calliope; Annabelle Montgomery, soubret, producer and chorus; Mary Wagner, characters and chorus; and Hazel Reynolds and Pearl Houston, chorus.

Vaudeville specialties are offered by Hazel Reynolds and Annabelle Montgomery, the "Majestic Sisters," in song and dance; Mary Wagner, cartoonist; Victor LaZelle, balancing; Houston and Gray, singing, dancing and talking; Catherine Reynolds, contortionist; Hazel Reynolds, singer; and the Musical Montgomerys."

That spring dawned bright and prosperous for us and the other showboat operators touring the Ohio and Mississippi River Systems. Showboats were more popular than ever due to the showing of the movie "*Showboat,*" in movie houses all over the country. Work was plentiful and everyone seemed to have money, and wanted to spend it.

The long awaited canalization of the Ohio River was completed in 1929. Forty-nine locks and movable dams were erected by the government to provide a nine-foot channel depth and keep the river open for uninterrupted travel. There were no more sandbars reaching halfway across the river, and no sandbars lying unseen under the water, to run aground on.

Reaching another milestone in my growth on the river, I began learning to play the calliope. All of us kids took a special interest in some phase of the business, and in addition to my acrobatic act, the piano and calliope were mine.

It was unthinkable for a ten year old girl to want to play such an instrument, but I did. I developed a good ear for music at an early age, and with Hazel or Tommy pumping the organ for me, I could play any tune I heard. Edith Hunter took me under her wing and taught me chords and how to read and write music.

One day when I was seated at the organ playing "Here Comes the Showboat," and "Over the Waves," with strong emphasis on the omm-pah-pah bass, Dad came into the dining room and told me, "I could hear you playing outside. It sounded pretty good."

"Like a calliope playing?" I asked.

"Yes, it did, but the calliope is a lot harder to play than the organ. Would you like to try playing one of your songs on the calliope this evening when I get up steam?" he asked.

"Yes!" I eagerly replied.

"All right, but first I want you to go with me to the calliope so I can explain how it works."

So I followed him to the roof deck of the *Atta Boy* where we stood looking down at the steam pipes, valves, graduated whistles, and copper wires connecting them to the tiny, 32 whistle keyboard.

As he pointed out, "All the whistles have double poppet valves pitched to produce the notes of the scale. When you press a key it opens the valve, releasing steam into it, and the proper note sounds. You can't skip your fingers over the keys like you do the piano or organ. If you do, the whistles will blow off-key. There's a time lapse of a few seconds before the note sounds. Remember to play slow and push the keys all the way down against the pressure,"

"I will," I replied and repeated the instruction to him, "Push the keys all the way down and play slow."

"The calliope is a beautiful sounding instrument when it's played correctly, and the worst sounding when it isn't. It takes a special person to master it. I've seen big strong men back away from it because of the steam pressure, the whistles hurting their ears, or they couldn't adapt their fingers and music to the narrow keyboard. That's why some of the calliopes we hear sound off-key, or the music runs together and we can't tell what tune they're playing. I've had dainty women who were some of the best calliope players on the river," he emphasized.

"Edith was a good calliope player," I said.

"Yes, she was. One of the best," he agreed.

"I'd like to be able to play like her someday," I told him.

"You can if you work at it," he said.

After having me stand in front of the calliope, and placing my hands on the keyboard, he told me, "You're not quite tall enough to apply enough pressure on the keys. I'll build a platform for you to stand on."

So that evening my big moment came at "Calliope time." I went with Dad and Charles Montgomery and watched him play several selections before he turned it over to me. By that time a large crowd had gathered on the riverbank listening to the music.

Dad placed the platform in front of the keyboard, then adjusted the steam to the lowest, sixty pounds, steam pressure and motioned for me to begin playing.

I took a deep breath, and with all the strength I could muster, I played the opening chord of "Over the Waves." What a thrill it was to see the dancing jets of steam belching forth from the whistles and hear the harsh, but pretty melody flowing from my fingertips, It was pure bliss!

Then my fingers became like putty and the music rapidly changed to an ugly mixture of broken chords, off-key whistle shrieks and mournful wails. The sound was positively awful! The dreadful noise could be heard from two-to-three miles away! Fighting back the tears of disappointment, I finally gave up and stepped back from the keyboard.

Grinning broadly, Dad told me, "That's not bad for your first try. You started out real good."

Giving me an affectionate pat on the head, Mr. Montgomery told me, "Catherine, you did fine. Your hands will be sore for a while, but they'll soon strengthen and get used to the steam pressure. You've got the right touch. Just keep working at it," he encouraged me. I received a nice round of applause from the people on the bank. Mr. Montgomery closed out the concert with "Down Yonder."

The noise I made learning to play the calliope would have driven anybody but my family up the wall. They were so pleased that I took an interest in learning to perform this important job for the boat that it was music to their ears.

Every morning Dad stopped the boat in some lonely spot along the river where I could practice my playing. It was usually in a wooded area. He went with me to the calliope and adjusted the steam and supervised my playing until time to be on our way again. My proud brother, Tommy, called it "Serenading the squirrels."

August 17, 1929. Uncle Tegie placed another ad in *"Billboard"* for a new cast of actors. It read:

"Showboat Majestic Wants – Teams, with specialties. State if double piano. Also calliope player. Long season. Six shows a week, two bills a season. Like a vacation. New Richmond, Ohio, 15th, Constance, Ky., 16th, North Bend, Ohio, 17th, Petersburg, Ky, 20th. Address Nicol and Reynolds."

The *Showboat News* reported August 25:

"The *Majestic* showboat operated by T. J. Nicol and Tom Reynolds, stopped at Constance, Ky., near Cincinnati, last Friday night and enjoyed fair business. In the lineup are T. J. Nicol and Tom Reynolds, owners and managers; Jack and Mayme Roberts, Billie Clark, Johnny Colman, Edith and Earl Hunter, Catherine, Hazel and Margaret Reynolds."

Six year old Margaret was making her stage debut as a dancer at this time. Annabelle coached her in a buck and wing dance and she made her little feet fly in the difficult steps. She was a born dancer, and always brought the house down. Soon she became a regular in the vaudeville lineup.

Edith and Earl Hunter didn't join the boat in the spring because they were expecting their second child. After their daughter was born they joined the showboat for the rest of the season with their two children. She spent hours teaching and encouraging me on the calliope. As soon as my hands were strong enough to play several songs, she let me play once every evening at concert time. "For experience in playing in front of a crowd," she told me.

The showboat calliopes, always called a cal-ee-ope by the river people, ranged from 21 to 32 whistles. The smaller the keyboard the more ingenuity was required to play it. As part of my training, Dad took me to all the other showboats that were playing near us. He'd ask the captain if I could try my hand at playing their calliopes. Surprised at my youth and interest in playing the instrument, they readily agreed and I put on a little show for them.

"For experience in playing other calliopes," Dad told me.

But now I know, that in addition to the valuable experience gained, it was his proud way of showing me off to the other showboat captains. They, for the most part, had trouble finding dependable calliope players for their boats, and Dad was growing his own.

I was the youngest person and only daughter of a showboat operator to play a steam calliope.

Chapter 9
Dad and Uncle Tegie Dissolve Partnerships

August 1929, Uncle Tegie told Dad that he and Aunt Ida wanted to retire and would sell him their half of the showboat and towboat for the $3,500 they'd put into the building of the boats. When Dad couldn't persuade them to change their minds the deal was closed with a gentleman's handshake, ending twenty compatible years of business together.

At this time the *Majestic* was a well established enterprise on the river and worth several times her original cost. She was popularly known as "the showboat with a spotless reputation."

The transaction took place just before the disastrous stock market crash of October 29, 1929, which plunged the nation into the Great Depression of the 1930's. We suffered heavy losses in the crash. Dad and Uncle Tegie both had stock in the new Roosevelt Hotel in Pittsburgh, and Government Bonds that were indefinitely tied up. Had it not been for the substantial amount of cash they kept on board for emergencies, and the summer's cash receipts not yet deposited in the bank, they would've been penniless.

After Uncle Tegie's brother, Dave Nicol, was killed in a Steeple Race in England, he sold his interest in several race horses. But they had money from the sale of their interest in the showboat, and Aunt Ida had jewelry and mink coats they could hock if things got desperate. Dad had the boats to see us through the hard times ahead.

Billboard – Nov. 9, 1929 – "T. J. Reynolds, who recently acquired his partner's interest in the *Majestic* Showboat, and who is now in full charge of the floating theatre, announces that he plans to keep the boat out as long as the weather permits. He states that he will remodel the *Majestic* this winter, and will start out next spring with a bigger show than he has ever had. The *Majestic* is now playing along the Green River to good business."

We continued showing and making every cent we could until mid-November, then rang down the curtain on the final performance of the season and tied up at Curdsville, Ky. for the winter.

Uncle Bill had also closed his show aboard the *America* on the Green River, Sept. 28, and tied up at Curdsville for the winter. The plays he presented were *"Call of the Woods,"* and *"Down on the Farm."* Twelve people were in the cast, including Uncle Bill and Ida Mae. She and Pauline also did a singing and dancing sister act.

Billboard, Oct. 5, 1929 – *America* Ends Good Season – Capt. William Reynolds Beats P.A. on Candy Sales Charge -

"At Brownsville, Ky., on the Green River, Capt. William Reynolds passed out 37 free tickets to the city officials and their wives. On the second night there he admitted the officials, but said the women would have to buy their tickets. All the city officials took the order good-naturedly, except one. He said that unless their wives were admitted free no candy sales could be held aboard the showboat. Reynolds went right on with the sales. In the meantime, the prosecuting attorney swore out warrants for Capt. Reynolds, and the two candy salesmen, charging them with operating a game of chance. He later changed the charge to Lottery.

When the trial came up, Reynolds' attorney pointed out that slot machines were being operated without any interference in the town and surrounding territory, also the local groceries were selling coffee and offering a premium with each pound. As a result of his argument, the official swore out three more warrants on the same charge. Uncle Bill filed a counter charge against him charging malice.

He had to go to another town to obtain his warrants, as the Brownsville judge refused to issue warrants against the boat or Uncle Bill. The deputy sheriff stated that even if the warrants were issued, he wouldn't serve it . . . and that ended it."

Dad received a warm welcome from the townspeople at Curdsville. Farmers extended their southern hospitality to Dad and the boys by giving them hunting privileges and all the popcorn and pumpkins left in their fields. One farmer said he would supply all the fresh milk, butter, eggs, smoked hams and plump stewing chickens we'd need at rock bottom prices. We also got our drinking water from his well.

The showboat kids received a warm welcome from the teachers and pupils at the little country schoolhouse. What a change it was from the big school we attended at Glenwood. The schoolhouse, a two story frame building, housed grades one through four on the first floor, and grades five through eight on the second floor. One teacher per classroom taught all four grades.

Miss Ruby Basham taught cousin Frank and me in the fourth grade, and Margaret in the first. Miss Ruby lived with her parents on a farm and drove to and from school by horse and buggy. The horse was kept tied outside the school door and the kids took turns feeding and watering it. There were 20 to 30 girls and boys of all ages in each room. The school was lit by reflector oil lamps and heated by a big potbellied coal stove. There was a Catholic School across the road.

Our schoolhouse served as a community center for town meetings and social gatherings. The showboat kids helped put on the entertainment, doing our vaudeville acts.

Fannie Belle Pane was my best friend. While visiting on her parents' farm I tried my hand at milking, churned butter, and bottle fed baby lambs. What a difference farm life was from the only one I knew on the river.

Orville Johnson, a boy in my class at school, son of Coast Guard Commodore Johnson, lived in a bungalow on the waterfront next to the boats. Sunday afternoon was open house to showboat kids and all the neighbors. We all gathered around the player piano and sang.

Beatrice Thompson, spinster daughter of the postmaster and owner of the General Store, also became a good friend. Her father had befriended us when mother died. She was lame and walked with crutches, but what a lovely talented person she was, skilled in all the domestic arts.

It wasn't long until her face became aglow with happiness. Uncle Bill began calling on her and she fell head over heels in love with him. The romance continued to blossom and they were married.

Her first wifely duty after moving aboard the *America* was to fire the cook and housekeeper, Anna Davis. This left Anna without a job stranded in a place that looked like it was a million miles from nowhere. Dad told Anna that we had plenty of room on the *Majestic*. If she would settle for room and meals until spring, he'd put her on the payroll as cook and ticket taker. So Anna agreed and moved aboard out boat where she was like one of the family for many years.

Meanwhile, Dad and Uncle Bill helped Uncle Tegie build a houseboat at the landing. It had a cross front room, a bedroom with adjoining bath – complete with stool and hand pump, a kitchen with built-in cabinets and sink with hand pump, pantry, and forward and aft decks. The only drawback was that the houseboat wasn't self-propelled. They had to hand pole it, or hitch a ride with another boat.

They moved off the *Majestic* with all their belongings, dogs and birds. It was sad to see them leave. Dad was very close to them. Ida was like a mother to him, and Tegie an older brother. Aunt Ida had kept everybody in line. If things didn't go to suit her, especially if the actors hit the bottle too much, or they broke the "no smoking" safety rules, she'd chew them out. "Put that in your pipe and smoke it!" she'd say, and when she really got mad she'd cuss like a sailor.

She later tole me, "Tom was a wonderful father to you kids after your mother died, but he wasn't a saint. There were times when I had to straighten him out too."

Dad, Garnett and Ruth moved into Tegie and Ida's vacated apartment. Hazel and I took the adjoining stateroom. Grandpa Francis Marion, who also retired from the business in 1929, came to live with us in his declining years. His room was on the back deck of the showboat.

His birthday was February 29, on leap year. When Garnett made him a birthday cake, his eyes got big and his face lit up like a little child's. "That's the first birthday cake I've ever had. But you put too many candles on it. My birthday only comes once every four years, so I'm only eighteen years old today," he teased.

"That's still a lot of candles, Pa," Dad told him.

"Yes, they represent a lot of years on the river and water over the dam for me," he said. "But looking back on my life, I wouldn't change it even if I could."

"Me neither," Dad agreed.

Grandpa was getting old and feeble, and suffered from terminal dropsy, but Dad and Uncle Bill still went to him for advice. He walked with a cane and was up and about most of the time. Sometimes a doctor had to tap fluid from his body. Bozo, his wirehaired terrier was his constant companion. He liked to sit on the back deck of the showboat with Bozo on his lap looking at the river scenery.

To make more room at the landing for the houseboat, Dad moved the *Majestic* and *Atta Boy* across the river. Then we rowed ourselves back and forth across the river in the skiff or rode the little one horse ferry. Except for the dirt ferry road leading down from the hill country to the landing, the riverbank on that side was walled up with tall cane grass and dense woods full of fruit, nuts, and maple sugar trees. Dad tapped some sugar maples near the boat and left buckets setting under the drainage spouts to catch the sap. It made delicious maple syrup for our pancakes.

One night Hazel and I were awakened by a prowler outside our stateroom. Then we saw a dark figure move in front of the window and stand up. It was large and appeared to be looking in at us. It nearly scared us out of our wits. Putting her hand over my mouth, Hazel said in a low whisper, "It's a bear! Don't make a sound, maybe it'll go away," then jerked me down under the covers. We laid there afraid to move or call out until daylight when the rest of the family was up and about.

Dad said, "Bears have never been known to come on a boat, you must've been dreaming or seen old Bum outside your window."

But, after looking around, he found Bum lying at the foot of the gangplank with his belly and sides ripped open. The bear had been attracted by the sugar sap and after eating his fill wandered upstairs aboard the showboat. The bear's footprints were found on the ground leading on and off the boat.

Bum, an Airedale terrier, was our guard dog. Every night after we'd gone to bed he had made his rounds to make sure all was well. We though he would die from the gaping wounds he'd received from the bear's claws, but Dad doctored them with axle grease and, using a household needle and thread, he sewed up the wounds. He soon had Bum back on his feet guarding us and the boats as usual.

The woods were like a supermarket in our back yard. If we wanted to make a pecan pie, hickory nut cake or walnut fudge, we just gathered the abundance of nuts. In places pecans were so thick we could shovel them up. Wild honey, apples, rabbits, squirrels and fish were also part of our menu.

Life was free and easy, we virtually lived off the land while we were there. The town was so remote from civilization we didn't see a stranger all winter. It was a wild and wonderful country. We relaxed and became one of the natives during our stay there. It was a mild winter with one light snow. Though the river was chilly, we bravely went swimming on sunny days.

That summer was the worst ever for live stage entertainment. Talking pictures were sweeping the country. Long lines waited outside movie theatres. Lower admission prices were offered movie-goers. So, one legitimate theatre after the other was going out of business, and hundreds of actors were out of work. Every town had a motion picture theatre or was building one.

Dad was lucky to have Garnett as his helper, Marion and Tommy as relief pilots, engineers, deckhands, part time actors, and advance agents for the boat. He had three girls working on the stage, out front, and behind the scenes. Having a large family actively learning every part of the business paid off. We were his greatest asset.

Dissolving partnerships with Aunt Ida and Uncle Tegie couldn't have happened at a better time. We could play to smaller crowds and still make a profit.

We received a bushel of mail from out-of-work actors in response to our spring ad in the *Billboard*. The actors accepted a fifty percent salary cut from $30 a week to $15 per team, plus room and board, and were happy to have steady work for the summer.

The usual three married teams and two single actors were hired and given the date to join the boat. Uncle Bill's actors were scheduled to arrive at the same time. There was no bus or packet service between Curdsville and the train station in Owensboro, Ky. They had to make the overland trip any way they could.

Dad and the boys made repairs, scrubbed, scraped, and painted the boats. Then they replaced the Old Nicol and Reynolds insignia on the showboat's pilothouse with T. J. Reynolds, and put the initials T. J. on each side of the *Atta Boy's* pilothouse.

The actors came into town by horse and buggy, on hay wagons and on foot. Curtains parted as ladies of the town looked to see the kind of clothes, makeup and hairdos the actresses were wearing. The young boys and oldtimers met them and showed them the way down to the *Majestic* and *America* showboats.

Dad made two trips ferrying our actors and their baggage across the river to the boat. They included Earl Whitaker, Director of the show, characters, piano and calliope player; Yvonne Whitaker, Kenneth and Marie Keim, Billy and Alma Van, Lena Dunbar, and Clifford Science, son of Anna Davis.

Before rehearsals of the play *"Lena Rivers,"* got underway, Dad called the family together and told us, "We are going to be facing some hard times. With Ida and Tegie gone the actors outnumber us on stage and they might try to get the upper hand. I want you to sit in on rehearsals and learn the lines to their parts in the play, vaudeville acts and bits. Be ready to take their place if any of them should get drunk, jump the show, or have to be laid off. Their salary and food is our biggest expense. The main thing is to keep going. If we continue to learn and perform the important jobs as a team we will make it through the depression."

My last day of school I bid my classmates and Miss Ruby goodbye and picked up my report card promoting me to the fifth grade. Fannie Belle and I promised to keep in touch.

The saddest time was when we had to tell Aunt Ida and Uncle Tegie goodbye. Uncle Bill and Beatrice had left early to open their show. When it was time for us to go, Dad didn't want to leave Ida and Tegie behind.

"Tie your houseboat alongside the *Atta Boy* and come along with us," he told them.

"No thanks, we appreciate it, but we want to stay here awhile longer so I can fish," Tegie said. "But let us know when you will be coming back this way and we'll hitch a ride with you to Cincinnati."

So, with Dad in the pilothouse and the rest of us on deck waving farewell to them, we started out on our next tour.

To my knowledge, the *Majestic* and *America* Showboats were the only showboats to spend a winter at Curdsville. The larger showboats couldn't make it that far upriver. So, we gave the oldtimers who sat around the potbellied stove in Thompson's General Store something to talk about long after we were gone.

Cargo of Memories

Chapter 10
The Great Depression

A nice crowd turned out for opening night at Spottsville, Kentucky, March 28, 1930. The new admission prices were – Reserved seats . . . 50¢, Balcony . . . 35¢, Adult general admission . . . 25¢, and children under 12 . . . 15¢. Garnett was in charge of the ticket office and sales. Anna was the ticket taker, Hazel and I usherettes. Dad, Marion and Tommy worked behind the scenes.

Billy Van made the opening announcement. Then following a 15 minute overture, the curtain went up on the show. Departing from the usual custom of sandwiching vaudeville between the first, second and third acts of the play, the drama *"Lena Rivers,"* was presented in it's entirety without interruption.

Intermission, with piano and drum music flowing from the pit, and prize candy sale was next. Billy held up one of the envelope size boxes of candy and told the audience, "Now we're going to sell you some candy. It's ten cents a box. In every box there is a small prize, and in every tenth box a numbered coupon for one of the larger prizes on stage. Everybody is a winner! Now, who wants the first box?"

Hands went up over the theatre and the sale was on. Patrons went crazy spending their last dime, or in some cases dollar, buying up to ten boxes at a time. Those finding a coupon in their boxes hurried up to the stage to claim their prizes.

A full-length vaudeville revue, augmented by five chorus girls in line, was presented during the last half of the show. The lineup included a saxophone solo by Clifford Science; Hobo comedy bit by Billy and Alma Van; Blues song "She May Be Somebody's Baby," and recitation by Lena Dunbar; "The Charleston," dancing by Hazel Reynolds; song duet with piano accordian accompaniment by Earl and Yvonne Whitaker; Chalk Talk Artist by Kenneth and Marie Keim; and grand finale number, "So Long, We'll See You Again."

In spite of the good show we had, and no matter how well Marion and Tommy billed the boat, our crowds continued to drop off due to the depression. All the showboats were out in full force vying for the trade, and all were singing the blues. Money was tight. People didn't have the money to come to the show, or were afraid to spend what little they did have on entertainment.

Coming to the Tennessee River junction we headed upbound on it hoping to find more ready cash at farming towns along its course. It was our first trip up the river and Dad didn't know anything about navigating it, or where the towns were located. All he had to go by was his years of experience, intuition, and a list of towns given to him by Captain Bill Menke. Our advertising posters and passes to the show were sent ahead via the small Mail Boat. Postmasters at the towns put them up for us.

The Tennessee River is 652 miles long. It is formed by the Holston and French Broad Rivers above Knoxville, Tennessee and flows through sections of Tennessee, Alabama, Mississippi, and Kentucky. It empties into the Ohio River at Paducah, Kentucky.

Gilbertsville, Kentucky, was our first stop. The patrons had to walk a narrow wagon road through swamps to get to the river. The ferry and watchman's cabin at the top of the hill was all that was visible of the town from the boat landing.

Sharing some of the landings with the packet *Tennessee Belle,* we continued making stops at towns in Ky., then in Tennessee. At Pine Bluff, we played to an overflowing crowd. The people came from everywhere. At Fort Henry, where Grant's men came in their gun boats during the Civil War, we picked up a basketful of Indian relics off the riverbank and in the cotton fields. Included was a tomahawk Dad kept on display in the ticket office.

At Reynoldsburg, some of our relatives came down to the boat to visit and see the show. At Daniel, my brother, Carl Jackson Reynolds, was born aboard the *Majestic.* Garnett was attended by the country doctor.

At Savannah the sheriff stopped Earl Whitaker from taking pictures of a sow with her piglets roaming the street under their Open Range Law.

Most farm people of that time didn't trust banks and weren't too affected by the stock market crash. They had hidden their savings, and not only had the money to come to the show, but were starved for entertainment. Everywhere we stopped, a good paying crowd turned out for the show. One of the oldtimers told Dad that the *Majestic* was the first showboat to come up the Tennessee River in years.

The Tennessee River was beautiful, like a jungle river with the Cumberland Mountains in the background. The quaint little towns looked like western movie sets with their dirt streets, hitching posts, watering troughs, livery stables and blacksmith shops. The riverbanks had dense vegetation, stately willows, white pine, cottonwood, and cypress trees. Sometimes cypress roots extended 12 to 15 feet above the ground. The river was still in its natural state before the TVA Act turned the valley into a land of lakes.

We didn't know the malaria carrying mosquito inhabited the area until Marion fell ill with the shakes and fever. At night, when the theatre lights came on, they swarmed down out of the trees to stage their attacks on us. We slept with tents of netting over our beds at night.

Mayflies, or willow bugs, were also a nuisance, but harmless. They swarmed by the millions. They fluttered around the lights and then dropped dead or dying to the floor. Like delicate snowflakes they piled up several inches deep on the decks, theatre, and on stage. We crushed them underfoot and slipped and slid as we performed. Finally, we had to take time out at least twice during the evening to clean them off the stage and out of the footlights before the show could continue. Morning found their dead carcasses piled everywhere.

Then there were the snakes! We saw big, black reptiles six to eight feet long. They were swimming in the river, lying stretched out on logs, and hanging in the shade of overhanging tree branches by the boats. Instead of running away from noise, even the loud calliope playing, they were strangely attracted by our presence at the landings.

"They are cottonmouth water moccasins and deadly poison," a man from one of the towns told Dad. He went on to warn him, "The cottonmouth is an aggressive snake. They have been known to strike swimmers under water, and to run down a man on land and bite him in the seat of his britches. So, be on the lookout for them, and stay away from them."

But they didn't keep us from playing and swimming in the river, or for me to take my daily swim back and forth across it with Dad rowing along side of me in the skiff. By now every river we traveled was a challenge for me to swim across and the snake infested Tennessee was no exception.

I helped Marion, Tommy, and Clifford build a one-man kayak. They constructed the framework while I sewed and fitted the muslin cover, then helped waterproof it with several coats of oil paint. We took turns riding in the kayak. The slightest move and we'd turn over. We were upside down in the water more than on top of it, but we soon got the hang of it and had wonderful times riding up one side of the river and down the other. One day I counted 84 snakes lying on the rocky shoreline as I passed by in the kayak. I wasn't afraid of them. It was just a natural part of my growing up on the river and I loved every minute of it.

I also enjoyed taking hikes through the woods and mountains with Hazel picking wildflowers. I went with Tommy to find fish bait for the trotline. We walked through tobacco fields catching big juicy worms off the plants, and waded through shallow creek beds looking under the rocks for crayfish. When we lifted up a rock, it stirred up the mud and we couldn't see what was under there. We just grabbed whatever moved, and one day I grabbed up a snake. I let out a scream that could be heard back at the boat, and it scared the snake as much as it did me. Throwing it down, I told Tommy, "I'm quitting!"

"Aw, Caty, those little snakes won't hurt you. Besides that's what we catch the big ones on," he said. So, I continued to help him.

Anna was a fine cook and friend to the family and crew. She also helped Garnett with the children, and washed and ironed the actor's white shirts for a small pittance. She was also a member of the Salvation Army and worked as a live-in housekeeper for well-to-do families in Parkersburg, West Virginia during the winter. A fine seamstress, she taught me how to adjust dress patterns and the finer points of sewing. I also learned how to knit and crochet.

I bought material for ten cents a yard at the general stores. For twenty five cents I made a sundress, matching cover-up and sun hat, and had them in all colors, one for each day of the week. I wasn't allowed to go uptown alone to shop, so when Garnett couldn't go with me, Anna did. She also took Margaret and me to church every Sunday evening.

Pittsburgh Landing, Tennessee, site of the Shiloh National Military Park and Cemetery, was our last upbound stop, 198 miles above the mouth of the Tennessee River. Dad had scheduled our visit there on Decoration Day when all the old soldiers, their families, and visitors were there to see the park and cemetery.

Margaret and I went with Dad to see the cemetery, just up the hill from the boat. We walked along the pathways looking at the officer's monuments, then the hundreds of soldier's graves marked by long rows of white crosses topped with small Confederate and Union Flags. It was a grim reminder that one of the bloodiest battles of the Civil War ahd been fought here.

Dad told us, "We had relatives who fought on both sides of the war. John Reynolds, a Union soldier, was camped here with his company guarding this side of the river. The Rebs were holed up with plenty of food on the other side and the Union army didn't have much food at the time. So, one night, John slipped over to the enemy's side, overtook the guard, stole a gunnysack of potatoes from their supplies, and swam back across the river with them on his back."

Returning to the boat, Dad was kept busy popping corn and selling it to the visitors coming down to see the boat. Though I was just learning how to play the guitar, I boldly sat on the nearby checkpost and charged a quarter to sing and play their song requests.

On our return trip downriver the play, *"Just Plain Folks,"* with new vaudeville revue was presented. Then we made a tour of the nearby Cumberland River to Paris Landing, Tennessee, and back.

Traveling back upbound on the Ohio we played to slimmer crowds. Except for the farming towns, where we sometimes took food in exchange for tickets to the show, the economy had sunk to an all-time low.

Aunt Ida and Uncle Tegie were waiting with their houseboat at the mouth of the Green River. They had paddled, drifted, and poled the boat twenty eight and one-half miles for the rendezvous. What a happy reunion! We tied their houseboat alongside the *Atta Boy* and transported them to New Port, Kentucky. There the houseboat was moored at the foot of Park Street, where they planned to stay.

Aunt Ida hung out her "Canary Birds for Sale" sign while Uncle Tegie went back to betting on the horses.

By now it was mid August. All the showboat operators who found they couldn't meet expenses playing one-night stands, with their high overheads, started playing stock at the larger cities for the first time. *Bryant's* Showboat was tied up at the foot of Lawrence Street at Cincinnati, the *Goldenrod* at Pittsburgh, and the *Hollywood,* formerly the *Columbia,* at Louisville. Up to this time license to show the large cities had been too high for the showboats to stop. It was now lowered on their behalf, and with the Fire Department helping to bring out the crowds for ten percent of the proceeds, they played to good business every night.

It was at this time that Dad received an offer from the Martin and Wilson Stock Company in Cincinnati that he couldn't turn down. So, he closed the present show and leased the *Majestic* to them for the remainder of the season. The 17 people show under the direction of Rube Martin, producing comic and playwright; A. F. Wilson, financier; and George Dunn, Agent.

With us staying in the background, they did everything from cooking their own meals, doing the laundry, to managing the business affairs and putting on the shows.

Presenting one of Martin's own mystery dramas, *"Fangs of the Rattler,"* and specialties augmented by eight chorus girls in elegant costumes in line, they played one week at Portsmouth, two weeks at

Huntington, two days at Point Pleasant, and Charleston, W. Va. for a three-week closing stand to good business. We kids attended schools there until the show closed in late October.

Back at Point Pleasant, with us staying on board, the *Majestic* was taken out on Gardner's Docks for new bottom planks and gunnels. It was a bad time to have to spend the $500, but necessary to keep her in good running condition.

Many changes had taken place since we had spent the winter here in 1927. The once booming little city was paralyzed by the depression. Heads of families were out of work with no prospects of finding other employment.

Hazel, who had won the admiration of thousands on the stage with her singing, dancing, cornet playing, and ingenue roles, eloped with Charles Bates and set up housekeeping at Point Pleasant. Charles was a licensed steamboat fireman and was one of the few lucky people who still had a good paying job. He was also Garnett's uncle.

Grandpa died aboard the *Majestic* on November 1, 1930. He became seriously ill and Dr. Barbee was called to the boat. Dad, Uncle Bill, Great Uncle John and Aunt Rachel, a preacher, were there. Aunt Rachel had been trying to convert Grandpa to the Christian faith for a long time and this was her last chance.

"Francis Marion, you are dying! Accept Jesus Christ as your Savior. Ask him to forgive your sins, or you're going straight to hell!"

Getting no response, she dropped to her knees by his bedside and began praying loudly, "Oh God, Our Father in heaven, have mercy on Francis Marion. Save him before it's too late."

Giving Dad a pitiful look, Grandpa weekly told him, "Tom, get here out of here, and let a man die in peace." And that he did shortly afterwards.

With the choir singing "Sweeter As the Years Go By," and all the family and his old cronies present, the funeral was held in the Church of God, at the top of the hill. Burial was made in Lone Oak Cemetery north of town.

Catherine Mae King, who lived in a new house on the waterfront became my best friend that winter. The daughter of Revena and Vada King, she had two younger sisters, Velma and Emogine, and a brother Revena, Jr.

Catherine liked to sew, so we spent a lot of time together making Aunt Jemima dolls, calico cats and dogs, pillows, and hooked rugs.

One day, while visiting me aboard the boat, Catherine asked, "Did you ever put a note in a bottle and throw it in the river for someone to find?"

"No," I said.

"Let's try it and see if we get an answer," she eagerly replied.

Getting pencils, paper and bottles with corks, I ask her, "What should I say in my note?"

"Tell who you are, your age, and what you do on the showboat." Then when she finished writing, she asked me, "How does this sound? Dear friend, I am thirteen years old and have black hair and brown eyes. I am one of four children in my family. I enjoy cooking and sewing. If you would like to be my pen pal, please write to me. Miss Catherine Mae King, 1003 First Street, Point Pleasant, West Virginia."

"It sounds good. Now, listen to mine," I said. "Dear finder of this note, I am the daughter of Captain Thomas Jefferson Reynolds, owner of the *Majestic* Showboat. I am 18 years old and have red hair and blue eyes. Perhaps you have seen me perform when we stopped at your town. I play all the leading roles in the plays, sing and dance in the vaudeville revue, and play the piano and calliope. I would love to hear from you. Miss Catherine Reynolds, *Majestic* Showboat, Point Pleasant, W. Va."

Giving me a shocked look, she asked, "Since when have you been eighteen years old and playing all the leading roles in the shows?"

"Since now, to make a bigger impression on whoever finds my bottle," I replied.

Going on deck we kissed the bottles for good luck, and pitched them in the river. The current quickly swept them out of the mouth of the Kanawha into the Ohio River. Then we began the long wait of watching the mail for an answer.

Harry King carried my books and walked home with me from school every day. He was Catherine Mae's uncle. One day he said he'd like to take me to the movies, but didn't have any money.

I had money, so on Saturday we slipped off together and went to the movies. I bought the tickets and popcorn. We had so much fun sitting there munching corn and holding hands that we lost track of the time and watched the movie twice.

Dad was waiting for me when I got back home and said, "Catherine, Tommy said he saw you and Harry together at the movies this afternoon. Is that true?"

"Yes," I didn't deny it.

"Harry's a fine clean-cut boy and comes from a good family, but you're not old enough to date. When you are, and the boy is man enough to come to me and ask my permission first, then I'll let you go. Until then, I don't want you slipping off with Harry or any other boy," he said.

I continued to see Harry at Church and at Catherine's house. My brother Tommy was always nearby, listening and watching, and keeping close tabs on me. And so, the winter quickly passed, spring arrived, and it was time to go on tour again.

Chapter 11
Staying Afloat in the Hard Times

The show opened April 6, 1931 at the city wharf, in Point Pleasant. Charging 15¢ and 35¢ admission for any seat in the theatre, a near capacity crowd turned out for the opening performance. Harry was sitting in the balcony.

With Kirk at the piano, Clifford on sax, and Tommy beating out the rhythm on the drums, the "12th Street Rag, Johnson's Rag, and Tiger Rag," flowed from the pit, getting the show off to a rousing start.

The curtain went up on the opening scene of *"Sputters the Stuttering Cowboy,"* starring DeWitt Kirk in the title role. We didn't know it yet, but Kirk hit the bottle between scenes and the more he drank the funnier he got. The crowd didn't just laugh at his stuttering, they howled with laughter and applause every time he came on stage.

I had the ingenue role and Tommy debuted in his first part.

Following intermission and the prize candy sale, the girl's chorus, Lena Dunbar, Kathryn Kirk, Alma Van, and Marie Keim opened the vaudeville revue singing and dancing to "Everything's Hotsy Now."

A comedy song and dance, "Will You Love Me When My Flivver is a Wreck?" by Toby Veva; a comedy bit "You Can't Take it With You," by Billy and Alma Van; a saxophone and clarinet solo, by Clifford Science; a knife throwing exhibition with Kenneth and Marie Keim; song and dance, "The Old Soft Shoe," by the Reynolds Sisters, Margaret and Catherine; a blues song, "Some of These Days," by Lena Dunbar; a Russian dance by Tommy Reynolds, Jr.; and a piano solo by DeWitt Kirk filled out the show.

Performing from the pit, Kirk played "There'll Be A Hot Time In The Old Town Tonight." He told the audience, "I had a friend who played the piano. His name was Sam. He only knew one song, but could play it to fit any occasion. He was frequently asked to play for dances. If it was a hoedown, he played it like this," and he banged it out in country music style. "If it was a waltz, it sounded like this," and played it in three-quarter time. "And if it was a tango, this is the way it sounded" and he played it with Latin American tempo.

"When Sam's friend got married he was asked to play for the wedding," and he played it like a sentimental ballad. "When Sam died I was asked to play for the funeral. In fitting tribute to him, I did it this way," he said, and played "There'll Be A Hot Time In Old Town Tonight," in solemn manner. The yelling, "Take him away!" he went crazy running his fingers up and down the keyboard, playing it "showboat style," meaning loud, fast, and jumping with rhythm, until he brought down the house with roaring applause.

After the curtain fell, I went to the front of the theatre to help bid the crowd goodbye. Harry came to the foot of the balcony stairway and waited until the last patron left, then ran over and kissed me on the cheek. This was the first time he'd kissed me and he did it with Dad, Garnett, and Margaret watching. He planted the kiss and ran out the door so fast I didn't even have time to say good-bye.

On the Kanawha and Upper Ohio river we took in scrip at coal mining towns and exchanged it for 90 cents on a dollar. The coal mines were closing down.

At larger towns we played two day engagements. *"Sputters the Stuttering Cowboy"* was presented the first evening, and *"The Fighting Parson"* the next.

In the farming areas along the Ohio, we took in some farm produce in exchange for tickets for the show.

At Jeffersonville, Indiana, Dad came to me and said, "Catherine, I was just talking to a fine looking man who came down to the boat looking for you."

"What on earth for," I asked with surprise.

"He found the note you put in a bottle, while fishing below the Falls, and was so impressed with what you had to say, he wanted to meet you," he replied. The bottle had traveled 438 miles.

"What did you tell him?" I was almost afraid to ask.

"That you weren't available. Let this be a lesson to you," he sternly replied. "You don't have to resort to such tactics to get the boys' attentions. You have enough of that already. You have to be careful of what you do or say, or you'll give someone the wrong impression."

That was the last note in a bottle I ever put in the river. Catherine never heard from her note.

My little brother, Jack, was cute as he could be tottering around on his fat bowed legs and getting into everything. A typical boy. One day while I was on the upper front deck of the showboat talking to Garnett, he climbed on a chair by the fence railing. He liked to bounce up and down on things and the next thing we knew, he had bounced himself over the railing and into the river two decks below. We had taken our eyes off him for only a moment, but that was enough. Hearing the splash and missing Jack, Garnett screamed, "Oh, my God! My baby!" and froze in her tracks.

I leaped onto the fence railing and dove into the river after him. I found him floundering around near the bottom and brought him back up to the surface fighting like a wildcat. It was all I could do to keep him from climbing on top of my head, pushing me down and drowning me. By now, Garnett and the rest of the crew were there on the bank to lend a hand. They all credited me with saving his life.

Marion, who had married Eloise Davis, and spent their honeymoon aboard the boat, was no longer with the showboat. Tommy took over his job as co-pilot, engineer, fireman, and advance agent. Twice weekly he went ahead of the boat to post bills, and didn't quit until every shop window and telephone pole had a show bill on it. He also went uptown and painted with washable white paint, SHOWBOAT TONIGHT 8:30 SHARP, and distributed handbills door to door. By now all the showboats, including the *Majestic,* had dropped their street ballyhoo and parade.

Business was bad, but we continued to make a profit because of our low overhead. Then we had a wreck while making passage through the Louisville and Portland Lock Canal. We had completed lockage and were moving out of the canal exit when the engine stopped and the showboat was swept into a rock piling along the shore.

"We knocked a hole in the gunnel, we're taking in water!" Tommy shouted up to Dad.

Pumping the emergency whistle Dad tore down from the pilothouse. He grabbed a feathertick mattress off one of the beds, went down inside the hull to stuff it into the hole. The damage extended below the waterline near the bow of the showboat. The feathertick kept the water from coming in until Dad made on-the-spot repairs. A broken gasket had caused the engine failure. Dad replaced it and we were on our way again.

That fall we returned to Point Pleasant for the winter.

The following spring of 1932 the bottom had dropped out of everything. Millions of people were out of work. There was very little money. People were going hungry. Precious heirlooms and antiques were being sold at auction for what little they would bring to buy food and pay rent. Families evicted from their homes moved in with relatives or took to the streets and roamed the country looking for food.

"Prosperity is just around the corner. There'll be a chicken in every pot," President Hoover promised, but the crisis continued.

We opened the season with the play "St. Elmo." Clifford Science starred in the title role and Lena Dunbar had the female lead. Other players were DeWitt Kirk, Kathryn Kirk, Toby Veva, Hap Moore, Billy Van, Alma Van, Billy and Anna Finnigan, the daughter of an Indian chief who went by the stage name Princess Omar. Tommy and I had supporting parts. Margaret and I also did a tap and acrobatic dance routine, and Tommy did buck and wing and Russian dancing.

It was a fine show, but few people had the price of a ticket to see it. Towns that once flourished and could support one showboat after the other had taken on a ghost like appearance with most of their business districts boarded up. The larger the town, the longer the soup and bread lines. The riverbanks were lined with shanty towns, called "Hoovervilles." The unemployed and their families lived side by side with hoboes in driftwood and cardboard shelters. The fish they caught from the river was sometimes all they had to eat.

It was sad to see the people who had never missed a show standing on the riverbank listening to the calliope concerts until show time, then turning around and going back home. Dad invited the boys standing on deck in free to see the show.

It was 105 degrees and not a breath of air stirring the morning we pulled in beside the ferry landing at Foster, Ky. "Let's run out some extra lines while we're at it, conditions are just right to get a storm before long," Dad told Tommy, Clifford, and Bones, our new deckhand.

Dad took me to see Norman's grave. It was a short walk from the boat landing to the graveyard at the top of the bank overlooking the Ohio River. It had a dozen or so monuments partially hidden by underbrush. Pushing weeds aside he went over to one of the graves and told me, "This is Norman's. That's the marker I made out of driftwood and carved his name and dates on it." He stood there sadly looking at the little grave for a while and then began pouring out the heartbreaking story of that terrible night when the *Illinois* had burned here sixteen years ago.

"It must've been awful," I tearfully replied.

"Yes, it was the worst thing that ever happened to your mother and me. He would've been a fine son had he lived. You'll never know what it's like to lose a child until you've lost one of your own, and I hope you never do," he said.

Anna was ringing the dinner bell when we returned to the boat. About half way through the meal there was a loud crash of thunder and lightning downriver from us. Then we heard a low rumbling sound like a freight train coming upriver.

His face draining of color, Dad leaped up and ran out the door with Tommy, Clifford and Bones at his heels to batten down the hatches and tend the lines.

Garnett, with Jack in her arms, and Anna taking Ruth by the hand, we broke all records getting off the *Atta Boy* and across the narrow plank onto the showboat. We just stood there looking at the approaching storm.

"Get off the deck. Quick!" Dad shouted to us.

The stage door was open, so we darted inside just as the storm hit. The howling wind hit the stern of the boats and we began moving away from the landing. The back of the *Atta Boy* swung out snapping the lines. The front of the showboat rammed into the bank, ripping off the gangplank. We just kept going. The trees our lines were tied to toppled over and were dragged out into the river. The spring line slipped off the checkpost so fast it was of no help.

Grabbing the ship anchor on the head of the boat, Dad threw it overboard, knowing the moment he dropped it that he'd forgotten to put a line on it. Then, thinking he might be able to guide the boat upriver in the wind and waves, he made a beeline to the pilothouse, only to find the steering wheel jammed.

A line from one of the trees had caught up underneath the rudders and paddle wheel. Tommy worked his way back to the fantail and severed the line with an ax. Then he ran to the pilothouse for further instructions.

"I don't know what's keeping the *Atta Boy* afloat. Waves are rolling knee-high over the deck and water is coming in faster than we can pump it out," Tommy told Dad.

"We have to get the boats stopped somehow. At the rate we're going we'll soon be at the dam. There's a shallow place upriver aways. I'll try to nose the showboat over to it to slow her down. If I can get her in close enough to the bank, drop the spud and get a line out," Dad said.

Meanwhile, we had moved on through the auditorium to the theatre lobby where we stood shaking with fear and looking out at the storm. What a sight. Uprooted trees and wreckage were flying through the air. The showboat was turning and tossing in the waves like a ship without a rudder. Every time we dipped from one side to the other the waves rolled up over the deck and across our feet in the theatre.

Princess Omar screamed and dropped to her knees, oblivious of the water coming in, and began praying, "Save us, dear Jesus, don't let us die!"

Dad succeeded in guiding the showboat over the shallows and Tommy got a line out. With the spud digging into the sandy river bottom we came to a bouncing, skidding stop. The wind quit blowing. It shut off all at once, just like it started. Our emergency landing was on the Ohio side two miles upriver from Foster.

We were on the front deck looking at the havoc the storm had wrought along both sides of the river, when Dad came around the side deck and asked, "Is everybody all right? That was some ride. See those trees in the river at the end of our lines. Well, they were a blessing in disguise. They helped hold us back and kept us from wrecking."

We laid over at the emergency landing pumping out water, checking for leaks, cleaning debris off the boats, replacing broken windows, mopping up the theatre, and waiting for the waves to subside.

Then, with us and the boats no worse for wear, we returned to Foster with Kirk at the calliope playing, "Here Comes the Showboat" again. There were more people out to greet us than before.

The town was untouched by the storm, but the riverbank was in shambles. Dad had to bury several timbers called dead men, with ringbolts for anchorage. The gangplank that had been driven into the shore mud when we hit the bank was dug out, washed off, and put back on the head of the boat. Dad and Tommy found the anchor with grappling hooks, and put it back in place on the front deck. We went on with the show.

An oldtimer shook Dad's hand before leaving saying, "Captain Reynolds that was a might fine show. Good enough to put on in a church. Thanks for bringing the showboat back so we could see it. We'd been looking forward to it, and would've been awfully disappointed if you hadn't."

Uncle Bill was touring the lower Ohio River with a medicine show. He sold half-pint bottles of "the remedy" which was guaranteed to cure everything from receding hairlines to fallen arches. He made it from river water and other secret ingredients. He had a candy sale and popcorn concession.

When we told him about our frightening experience, he laughingly said, "One night the *America* was blown loose in a storm when the people on board were watching the show. Thinking it was part of the entertainment they stayed in their seats watching. After a while, one of the men came to me and asked, "Captain Reynolds, when are you going to take us back?"

We tied up at Louisville, Ky., for a week engagement. There was a new city noise ordinance that prohibited us from playing the calliope. So, we set up loudspeakers and presented live music until curtain time. But, here again, in the city, people were the hardest hit by the depression. We played to less than half a house every night.

The movie "*Showboat,*" was playing in competition with us at the local theatre. The owner invited Dad to see the matinee showing of the movie, and when it was over, he asked Dad's opinion of it.

"It's a fine show," Dad told him, "But it's nothing like real showboating."

On the Tennessee River the people were suffering hardships from the three years of drought. The river was at its lowest level in years. Water for general use had to be carried and hauled in barrels by horse and wagon from the river. The domestic animals and wildlife looked like walking skeletons coming down to the river to drink.

They were also being invaded by the seventeen-year locust. The locusts swarmed down out of the sky like black clouds eating every leafy morsel in sight.

But most of the farmers still had enough food stored in sheds and fruit cellars to eat, sell, and trade for tickets to the show. We bought some of the sweetest cured hams from them at 40¢ each, bacon was 10¢ a pound, and fresh eggs three dozen for a quarter. At the stores we paid 25¢ a pound for coffee and 15¢ a pound for round steak. We had steak for dinner when we could find it. Anna cooked it so it would melt in your mouth.

With all of this, plus the fish we caught from the river and canned food Garnett had preserved in the showboat hull, we never lacked for good things to eat.

But others weren't so lucky. Everywhere we went we saw people in need. It wasn't unusual for a man and his family to come down to the boat at the towns and ask for money to buy food or medicine for one of the children who was ill. Dad never turned anyone away. He took in all the foodstuff the farmers brought to the boat and what we didn't need he gave to those who did need it. I also saw him give them money out of his own pocket.

At Pine Bluff, Tennessee, a large crowd turned out for the show. They came by the horse and wagon loads from back in the hills. They were having a wonderful time enjoying the show. Then the lights went out. Kirk came on stage with a flashlight and told them that the light plant broke down and he would give them their money back. Or, they could continue the show with lantern lights.

"Let's go on with the show!" voices rang out from the crowd. So we gathered up all our oil lamps and lanterns, and the men from the crowd brought their lanterns in off their wagons. Setting them across the front of the stage we went on with the show, presenting it in the old-fashioned way, and no one was disappointed.

"*Lena Rivers,*" was our alternate bill. The new acts were a "Ragtime Wedding," by Kirk, the jiving preacher, Billy and Alma Van: Solo "Down By The Winegar Woiks," and waltz clog dance, by yours truly, a tough kid in boys knickers; Monologuist, Toby Veva; saxophone solo and tap dance, "Fascination Rhythm," by Clifford Science; Trixie the Dancing Poodle and her trainer, Princess Omar; solo "The St. Louis Blues," by Lena Dunbar; solo "Now I've Got a Mother-in-law, from sucking cider through a straw," and eccentric dance, by Hap Moore; a competitive tap and Russian dancing, by Margaret and Tommy Reynolds, Jr., ended the show.

We made a round-trip tour of the Cumberland River as far as Paris Landing, Tennessee. Then we worked our way back up the Ohio in the fall.

At Utica, Indiana, after the show, Tommy, Margaret, and I combed the theatre as usual looking for discarded cigarette butts, and Dad doused the fire and hot coals in the boiler with water before coming upstairs to bed.

When all the lights went out, Pal, our young German shepherd watchdog, took his post at the head of the gangplank. Around two o'clock Pal woke Dad up barking and scratching at his balcony door. The room was full of smoke. Leaping out of bed he shook Garnett awake and told her, "The boat's on fire! Get everybody up! Quick!" With Pal barking excitedly and leading the way, he followed him down through the theatre to the back stage area where fire was shooting out of the hold and up the walls. He connected the fire hose to the automatic pump and sprayed water from the river on the flames. Moments later he was joined by Tommy, Clifford, and Bones.

Meanwhile, Margaret and I were awakened by Pal barking outside our door. Going from room to room with Garnett we pounded on the doors waking Anna and the actors. Then we all gathered in our night clothes on the upper back deck of the showboat near the stairway. We waited and silently prayed that the fire would be brought under control.

Finally, the soot covered form of my father appeared. He had been running around fighting the fire in his birthday suit! He slept in the nude, and in the excitement he'd forgotten to put on his pants. We all laughed with relief, and went back to bed.

The fire started underneath the boiler and spread through the hull and up through the floor into the back stage area. The most serious damage was to the new bottom planks we had just put on the boat. The dressing rooms, costumes, makeup and equipment was a total loss. Thanks to Pal, another tragedy like the burning of the *Illinois* was averted.

The show closed at Point Pleasant on October 15th. The *Majestic* was taken to Smith's Docks again for repairs to her hull due to the fire. It had been a poor season for us. There were times when we didn't make expenses and Dad had to dig down in his pockets to pay the actors. But, we never missed a night showing and ended the season in the black again.

We were lucky. Some of the grand old showboats didn't make it. Otto Hitner's fabulous *Cotton Blossom* was sold at auction for debts. Menke's *Sensation* was dismantled. William Hart's *Valley* was taken out of service after she sank. Out of the seventeen showboats that were on the river with us in 1924, only seven remained.

Bryant's Showboat was playing summer stock at Cincinnati, J. W. Menke's *Goldenrod* at Pittsburgh, and the Menke Brothers' *Hollywood* was at Alton, Illinois, charging 24¢ admission. This left only the *Majestic, America,* and *Water Queen* still carrying on the tradition of one night stands in 1932.

It was the cruelest year of the depression. The bottom had dropped out of everything that winter. There was a complete work stoppage. February, 1933, the banking system collapsed. The people looked to Franklin D. Roosevelt, our newly elected president, and his New Deal policies for economical and social change.

After a while, low interest loans to farmers helped get them back on their feet. He re-opened steel mills and factories. He built up the army reserves and created new construction jobs and conservation projects. Soon the Blue Eagle, symbol of the National Recovery Administration, was everywhere. Every shop window across America had a Blue Eagle on it. The depression had hit bottom, and we were starting to bounce back.

March 17th, water was running three to six feet deep through the streets of Point Pleasant. In the lowlands the people were run out of their second stories of their homes by the floodwater. Men in rowboats evacuated people from their shops and homes.

In Kingtown, Dad let the people move their furniture aboard the showboat, piling it on top of the theatre seats, along the aisles, and on the front deck of the showboat. he also let some of the families who didn't have anywhere else to go move into our vacant rooms, and use the kitchen facilities. They remained on board with us sitting amid the tree tops until the flood waters receded. Then they cleaned the mud out of their houses, disinfected, and moved back in with their belongings.

Soon the actors arrived. They were the erstwhile director of the show, DeWitt Kirk; Kathryn Kirk; and their teenage children, George and Gracie; Roy and Lois Sheets, who previously toured with the *America;* Clifford Science; Toby Veva, and Hap Moore.

Rehearsals of the comedy drama *"Huckleberry Finn,"* began. Roy Sheets had the title role and I had my first co-starring role of Becky Thatcher.

Gracie, Margaret and I went every evening to an evangelical meeting at the Church of God on the waterfront. Mark Shifflet was a fire and brimstone preacher and had an alter call every night. One night Catherine Mae, Harry, and I were saved.

On Easter Sunday the meeting came to a close with all the new converts being baptized in the Kanawha River in front of the showboat. It was cold outside and the river like ice. Dad let them use the ticket office and concession room for dressing rooms. With all the family and actors on the front deck of the showboat watching, Preacher Shifflet waded out in the river and one by one the converts were immersed.

With the Blue Eagle posted on the head of the showboat and Kirk at the calliope playing "Happy Days Are Here Again," we opened the show at Gallipolis, Ohio, April 23, 1933. We returned to Point Pleasant and showed the following day. From there we continued upbound on the Ohio River.

At Burlington, Ohio, we awoke to find the showboat tipped over sideways in the river. The river level dropped during the night and left the boat caught out on a steep ledge. Margaret and I were sleeping so soundly we didn't feel our bed scoot across the floor against the window. It was scary when we stepped out on the sloping deck and saw what had happened.

The boat was lying in a twisted angle with her portside on the ledge and her leeward side underwater up to the guard.

The *Atta Boy* was worked loose and Dad tried to pull the showboat back out in the river, but it wouldn't budge. An emergency call was made to the nearest locks to raise the water level. Then, with the boat floating free, we were off and running again.

Anna Davis was ill and couldn't make the tour with us that spring. Charles Wamsley, a professional steamboat cook from Point Pleasant, was hired in her place. A quiet man, Charley also took up tickets for the show.

One morning we pulled into Rices Landing, Pennsylvania, on the Monongahela River. Julia, a pretty Italian lady was standing on the bank, smiling and waving with the rest of the crowd. Well, Charley saw her, and it was love at first sight, a love that would last their lifetime. Three days later they were married. Julia then shyly joined him aboard the boat. We feted them with a wedding reception in the dining room and shivaree after the show.

Julia made nineteen people on board, counting my new baby brother, John Lewis, who had been born on the *Majestic* in the early spring.

Everywhere we went that summer there were visible signs of recovery. Though many people were still out of work, it was wonderful to see the factory smoke rising from the chimney tops again. The miners were going back to work. The steamboats came out of mothballs and resumed their cargo shipments along the rivers. Boards were removed from store fronts and open signs were hung. Soup lines were disappearing and the smiling faces of patrons started coming back to the showboat.

The *America* Showboat went out of business that summer. It needed a new hull, and rather than spend the money Uncle Bill beached her at Curdsville, Kentucky. Then he sold her for $50 for use as a club house. She was then sold to the Bluebird Pie Company in Owensboro, torn down, and the lumber used to build two rental cottages at Curdsville. Thus ending the career of this beloved showboat. The *Ida Mae* towboat wasn't included in the sale. But, with the demise of the *America,* only six showboats now remained in business.

Cargo of Memories

Captain Tom Reynolds and family about 1919.

Nichol & Reynolds' first showboat. Seated 220 people anunt Ida is on the upper front deck. Mother and Norman midway, and Marion at the back. Photo from postcard.

The *Liberty* in tow of the *Illionis*. Courtesy of Boat Photo Museum.

Francis Marion Reynolds. Family photograph

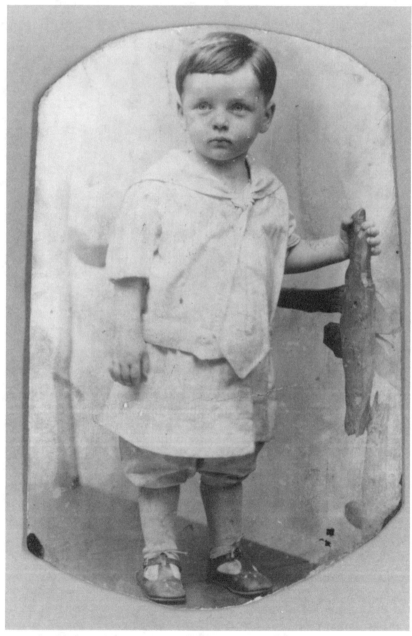

Norman Reynolds, who lost his life in the fire. Family photograph.

Nichol & Reynolds' second showboat. Seating capacity 300.
Courtesy Boat Photo Museum.

Reynolds and Son's showboat *Superior Theatre*. Built on the salvaged
hull of the *Illionios* showboat. Seated 200. The gasboat *Superior* was
formerly the *Kate Paden*. Family photograph.

Ida and Thomas Nichols, and their dog Queenie. A family
photograph made aboard Ben Raike's Photography Boat.

Nichol & Reynolds' third showboat. Seated 425 people. The
smaller *America* is lying alongside. Family photograph.

Interior of the *Majestic* in 1923. Family photograph.

Back view of the *Majestic* and *Atta Boy*. Photograph by author.

The "Point" at Pittsburgh, PA, where the Allegheny and Monongahela River, lower right, unites to form the Ohio River at the top of the picture. Courtesy of Carnegie Library of Pittsburgh.

At Fairmont, West Virginia, in 1933. That is Tommy and Clifford Science (in black) on the top deck. Gracie Kirk, Kathryn Degan Kirk, DeWitt Kirk, Margaret, the author (in white), Ruth, and Garnett with Baby John Lewis Reynolds in arms on the second deck. Dad (in straw hat), Charles Wamsley, Roy and Lois Sheets, and George Kirk on the main deck. Jack Reynolds (in bibbed overalls), and his five playmates from the town are on the gangplank. A placard picture.

Reading rehearsal of the 3-act play "Ace In The Hole" in the spring of 1935. Back row – Author, Harrison Finner, Eddie Kirk, Hap MOore, George Kirk, Gracie Kirk, Myrtle Degan. Front Row – Kathryn Kirk and DeWitt Kirk, Producer Director of the show. Courtesy of *The Pittsburgh Press.*

Family Portrait. Dad, Garnett, Ruth, Margaret and Catherine (age 15) and Pal. Courtesy of *Click's Guide Magazine.*

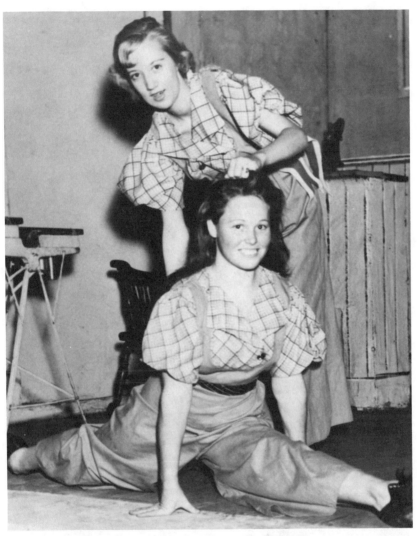

Gracie and the author practicing and acrobatic and tap dance routine. Courtesy of *The Pittsburgh Press*.

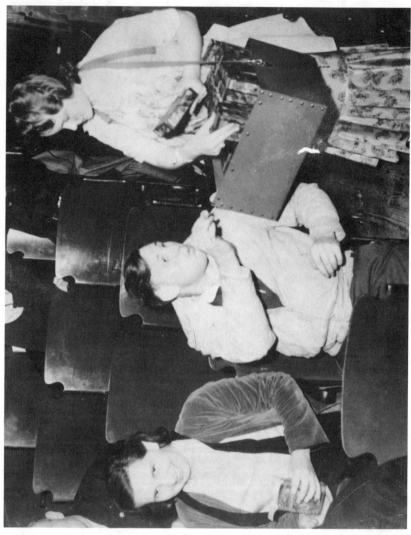

Catherine selling prize boxes of candy to a handful of patrons before our business picked up. Courtesy of *The Pittsburgh Press*.

The author is shown taking time out from her swimming to pose
for the camera. Family photograph.

Point Pleasant, WV, inundated by floodwater from the Ohio River on the left, and the Great Kanawha River on the lower right. Look closely and you can see the Majestic setting in the treetops between the W. Va. and the 1937 date, on the Henderson side. Courtesy of U.S. Army Corps of Engineers, Huntinton District.

Moving downbound through the Beverly, Ohio Canal in
August, 1941.

Backing broadside into the landing with calliope playing.

The excursion steamer "Senator," on which the author was guest calliopist during our visit to East Liverpool in 1941. Courtesy Frederick J. McCabe Liberty Marine Photos.

Moving under the Sixth Street drawbridge. Courtesy Clair C. Stebbens.

In Zanesville, OH, beneath the Fifth Street Bridge, at the Mast & Hann's private landing. Courtesy The Zanesville Times Recorder.

Margaret Catherine King sitting on deck outside our stateroom aboard the Atta Boy. Family Photograph.

Special dramatic presentation of the "Hatfields & McCoys." Sponsored by the Central PTA and put on by local talent for the B&O Railroad Officials who were in Point Pleasant for the dedication of their new Railroad Bridge on the Kanawha River, between Henderson and Point Pleasant, in July 1947. Courtesy Willis W. Cook.

Grand opening of the Kent State University Showboat at Point
Pleasant, June 7, 1948. The excursion boat Avalon was also there,
taking out daytime and moonlight excursions. Courtesy *The Dayton
Daily News.*

A quiet place on the canal. Family photograph.

Catherine at the keyboard. Family photograph.

Full house at Charleston, West Virginia. Courtesy U.S.
Associated Press.

At Charleston, West Virginia. Courtesy Cabot Inc.

Showboat parade moving up the hill at New Martinsville, West
Virginia. Courtesy *The St. Louis Post-Dispatch*.

The "River Players" at Charleston, West Virginia. Courtesy William E. Reed Collection.

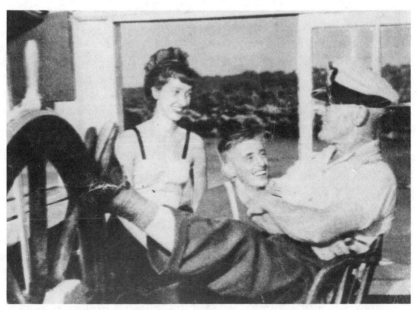

Captain Reynolds, spinning a yarn to two collegians as he navigated the boat with his foot. Courtesy *The Pittsburgh Press*.

Captain Reynolds taught a course all of his own in river and showboat lore. Courtesy *The Columbus (OH) Dispatch*. 1954

At Pittsburgh, PA, close by the legitimate Theatre District, in
August, 1957. Courtesy *The Pittsburgh Press*.

Townspeople going on board to see the show in 1957. Press book
photograph.

The *Majestic* making a Kroger television commercial at Pittsburgh in August 1958. That's Tommy (hands on hips) standing on the lower front deck with Kroger Officials and other dignitaries. Courtesy Photo Museum.

The box office is booming at every stop. Courtesy *The Indiana University Press.*

1961 — Second Season — June 8 - September 2

I. U. "SHOWBOAT, INC."
MAJESTIC

Presents

"PEG O' MY HEART"

A Comedy of Youth
By J. Hartley Manners

Cast

(in order of appearance)

Mrs. Chichester	Rose Marie Bank
Jarvis	Jon Wyatt, Jon Meyer
Ethel	Karen Brooks, Diana Menke, Andrea Rees
Alaric	Mike Keiter, David Edgerton
Christian Brent	Ken McGlon, David Edgerton
Peg	Judy Noble, Diana Menke
Mr. Hawkes	Jon Hedman, Jon Wyatt
Maid	Margaret Read, Andrea Rees
Jerry	Robert Berry

Scene: Mrs. Chichester's Living Room
Scarborough, England
Time: Summertime

(The curtain will be lowered in second act to denote passing of a few hours)
There will be two 10-minute intermissions

All Time, Old Time, Good Time, Prize Candy Sale

GALA VARIETY SHOW

ORCHESTRA

Piano	Margaret Read
Clarinet	Robert Berry
Trombone	Jon Hedman
Drums	Jon Wyatt, Mike Keiter

FACULTY, STAFF and CREW

Lee Norvelle	Executive Director
Richard Moody	Director of University Theatre
William E. Kinzer	Director Aboard
Hubert C. Heffner	Educational Director
Alice Nelson	Director of Housing
E. Ross Bartley	Director of Publicity
Captain Leon Ash, Captain Fred McCandless	Pilots
Art Graviss	Engineer
Robert Berry	Assistant Engineer
Tom White	Assistant Director of Publicity
Douglas Wilson	Advance Man
Martha McBride	Administrative Dietician
Annie Snowberger	Cook
Connie Waltz	Assistant Cook
Dorothy Beck	Business Manager, Chaperon
Duane Reed	Assistant to the Director
Margaret Read	Calliopist

Credit

THE RANGES AND GAS REFRIGERATOR ARE FURNISHED THROUGH THE COURTESY OF
WHIRLPOOL CORPORATION, EVANSVILLE, INDIANA DIVISION
I.U. "SHOWBOAT, INC." is strictly a non-profit organization, chartered
by the State of Indiana, with the following officers:

LEE NORVELLE, President   J. A. FRANKLIN, Vice-President and Treasurer
MRS. ALICE NELSON, Secretary

Indiana University Majestic Showboat handbill in 1961.

Majestic making her historic arrival at Cincinnati, Sunday, October 1, 1967. Courtesy *The Cincinnati Enquirer*.

The *Majestic* and *Atta Boy* lying at their permanent landing at the
Foot of Broadway, adjacent to the Riverfront Stadium, in Cincinnati,
Ohio, in 1968. Courtesy Cincinnati Bell, Public Relations Dept.

The *Atta Boy* as she looks now after being rebuilt from the hull up, following the fire that gutted her interior. Courtesy Miss Becky DImley, student photographer.

Circus wagon with the *Majestic's* old calliope playing during the staging of the 500 Festival Parade in downtown Indianapolis in May, 1976. Larry MacPherson, University at Indianapolis.

Chapter 12
Highlights of
1934–1935–1936 Tours

We opened the season at Point Pleasant on April 10, 1934, and continued upbound on the Ohio playing to much better business than the previous season. The comedy drama *"Just Sally,"* and five vaudeville acts were presented. I had the title role of Sally, and Clifford Science, the male lead.

I was used to young men whistling and flirting with me during the show, but one night I fell asleep with an admirer sitting on the riverbank singing love songs to me at the top of his lungs.

All the crew had heard him and gave me sly looks the following morning. Dad was the only one who came right out and asked me, "Did you hear that boy howling at the moon over you last night?"

"Yes," I replied.

"Boy, he sure had it bad," he said, grinning ear to ear.

The *Water Queen* Showboat wintered at Point Pleasant and also opened its season there. The Hyatt's engaged Uncle Bill, his family, and the *Ida Mae* towboat to work for them. Uncle Bill was the pilot, his sons Raymond and Frank, and Vernon Smoot, the Hyatt's nephew, were his helpers.

Uncle Bill also played comedy parts in their plays, trumpet in the pit, and performed his famous eccentric songs and dances. Ida Mae did parts in the play and singing and dancing sister acts with eight year old Pauline. She took up tickets and helped in the dining room and kitchen.

Ida Mae seriously told me, "Jossie Hyatt was very religious. She said grace before all our meals."

All went well until the *Water Queen* was involved in an accident. According to Jossie, a steamboat ran into them while pulling into the landing at Belle, W. Va. The impact weakened the boat's superstructure. This, plus Roy Hyatt's failing health, caused them to retire the showboat. They returned to Point Pleasant, at the Goosetown Landing, where the *Water Queen* went out of business.

It was love at first sight for Gracie Kirk and Jules LaPorte when he joined the showboat. A shipboard romance ensued, resulting with their marriage on stage.

The local minister didn't want to perform the ceremony on the showboat, saying it was sacrilegious. But, Gracie's father, Kirk, told him that he and Kathryn were married on stage aboard the Cooley and Thom's *Wonderland Showboat* twenty two years earlier. He said show business was a profession and not all actors were atheists. Finally, the minister agreed to marry them.

I sang "Sweethearts Forever" to the accompaniment of the band. The wedding ceremony was performed on stage after the show at Maidsville, West Virginia, June 4, 1934. It was the first showboat wedding remembered on the Monongahela River and the boat was packed for the occasion.

> *Billboard* – Cincinnati – August 11, 1934 – *"Majestic* Showboat on its way down the Ohio River played Constance, Ky., early last week and was visited by some members of the Billboard staff. Had about three fourths house, lower floor and balcony.
>
> The dramatic bill was the *"Boss of the Bar Z Ranch,"* in three acts, and cleverly presented, following which there were five specialty numbers including Clifford Science, saxophone and clarinet solos playing both instruments at the same time; Ray Barnes, banjo specialties; Kirk and Degan, comedy sketch; Gracie Kirk and Catherine Reynolds, songs and dances; Tommy and Margaret Reynolds, song and dance specialties. The show was warmly received by the audience.
>
> Captain T. J. Reynolds is owner, manager, and pilot; Tommy Reynolds, engineer. The play and specialties personnel also included Jules LaPorte, Kitty Kirk, George Kirk, and Glen "Popeye" Mullinax. Orchestra: DeWitt Kirk, piano and leader (Is also calliopist); Clifford Science, sax; Ray Barnes, banjo; and Tommy Reynolds, drums."

Billboard – Cincinnati – August 25, – "DeWitt Kirk, of *Majestic* Showboat, states that boat played Rising Sun, Indiana, day of dedication of the new City Hall. Governor McNutt was there for the day and Judge Ricketts made arrangements to have the parade pass along the riverfront. Kirk played steam calliope for the parade. City officials were kind to *Majestic,* announcing show from speaker's platform through loud speakers, also not charging any license for the show. Capacity business was done. Indianapolis papers took pictures of showboat."

Ray Barnes, or Barney, performed a novelty musical act. He played a handsaw with a violin bow, a washboard with thimbles, bells, whistles, inflated balloon, jug, comb, a bass fiddle made from a washtub, and a rack of water-tuned whiskey bottles.

Barney was also a very fine artist. He decorated the lower theatre walls with oil paintings. They included a life-size portrait of President Roosevelt sitting in a chair like the guest of honor next to the box seat compartment by the stage. Dad thought there was no one like Roosevelt and was proud to have his likeness on display for everyone to see.

The other paintings were a coal miner going to work with his dinner pail, a tabby cat floating down the river atop a barrel during a flood, a farmer tilling soil with mule and plough, a sunset scene on the river, and a family coming to the showboat.

He was also known as Barney the Piano Tuner. He tuned pianos at homes along the river. He gave all his money to the children playing on the riverbank. He never kept any of the money for himself, just gave it to the children who he felt needed it more than he did.

Everywhere we went that summer, on the Ohio, Monongahela, Kentucky and Tennessee Rivers, we saw an upswing in the economy. People had hope in the future again.

Billboard – Constance, Ky., October 27 – "T. J. Reynolds *Majestic* Showboat season closed here last night. Business this season has been considerably better than in the last several years, according to the management. Reynolds is taking the boat back to Point Pleasant, W. Va. for the winter."

The spring of 1935 Dad was painting the showboat when a lady came on board with her suitcase and typewriter. Thinking Dad was a hired hand, she asked him, "where can I find Captain Reynolds?"

"You're looking at him" he replied after a long silence. The boat was leaving in a couple of days and he was pressed for time, so he kept painting.

"I'm Bertha Wellman, reporter for the *Pittsburgh Press*. I've been assigned to write a series of articles about the showboat and would like to ride along with you when she goes upriver," she said.

"I don't know where I'll put you," he told her, with a twinkle in his eye. "There are no more beds. The only place would be with Anna, our cook. You'll find her upstairs in the kitchen aboard the *Atta Boy*. Just follow your nose around the side deck to the back. You can't miss it. Tell her I sent you."

After settling in, Bertha made the rounds of the boats to meet everybody. She sat in the balcony watching us rehearse the play. For a week she was like one of the family. She ate, talked, and dreamed showboating. She burned the midnight oil typing the stories she'd gleaned during the day. She even tried her hand at playing the calliope before flagging down the train back to Pittsburgh.

Jossie Hyatt was also a regular visitor, sitting in the balcony beside Bertha. I joined them between my rehearsal scenes. Saddened over not taking the *Water Queen* showboat on tour that spring, she reminisced about the thirty one years she and Roy had lived on the grand old showboat. She spoke of the time Gloria Swanson was on board for the filming of *"Stage Struck."* Once Roy had sold the *Water Queen* to Otto Hitner, who changed her name to *Cotton Blossom No. 2*. She had missed the showboat so much that Roy had bought it back for her to make her happy.

Beginning June 17, 1935, Bertha Wellman's illustrated articles began appearing daily in the *Pittsburgh Press*. They were titled "HERE COMES THE SHOWBOAT" and subtitled, "Romance Still Rides Colorful Flat Bottoms On Nation's Rivers."

A lavish picture layout of the *Majestic*, family and actors also came out in *Click's Guide Magazine* that summer. Because of all the publicity, we played to near capacity crowds at every stop. Everywhere we went that summer, on the Ohio, Monongahela, Kentucky and Tennessee Rivers, we saw an upswing in the economy.

Dad stood on the head of the showboat with a happy look on his face watching paying guests fill the theatre with their joyful presence again. For us, the depression had ended.

We presented the four act comedy drama, *"Ace In The Hole."* Gracie Kirk LaPorte had the lead and her brother, Eddie Kirk the co-starring role. Others in the cast were DeWitt Kirk, Kathryn Kirk, George Kirk, Myrtle Degan, Harrison Finner, Hap Moore, and myself.

We stopped at Rochester, Pennsylvania for a double engagement, and stayed two weeks due to popular request. The theatre was filled to standing room only every night and weekend matinees. We could've stayed there indefinitely, but promised we'd stop there again with a new bill, *"In Wyoming,"* on our return trip downriver.

We finished out the remainder of the season touring the Ohio, Cumberland, and Kanawha Rivers. Then we returned to Point Pleasant and bought a waterfront boat landing. It was located next to Charley Stone's ferry landing and the new Shadle Bridge, at the mouth of the Kanawha River. This was the same location where I was born and the *America* Showboat swept loose in the ice run of 1918. The landing is now owned by my brother Carl Jackson Reynolds.

The *Water Queen* Showboat, with the *Ida Mae* moored at the stern, was lying at the Goosetown Landing on the opposite side of the river. Uncle Bill was her caretaker.

The *Bryant* Showboat, in tow of the steamer *Valley Belle,* with Captain Billy at the wheel, and all the family on board, pulled into the vacant landing above us for the winter. They'd just closed their sixth season at the foot of Lawrence Street in Cincinnati.

The *Majestic* had been the only showboat playing the rivers, making stops at towns, in 1935. Saying he got as nervous as a cat staying in one place too long, Dad brought theatre to as many people as time would allow before closing the show for the winter.

With no new showboats being built to replace those that had gone out of business, and the remaining boats playing summer stock tied up to the dock at cities, an important part of our river heritage, and culture was fast fading away.

My brother, Roy, was born aboard the *Majestic* in 1935. In the spring of 1936, flood water flowed through the streets of Point Pleasant and Henderson, following the ice run. As the water started back down, Dad was kept busy pushing the boats out into the river to keep them from getting caught out on the bank. He checked the number of inches the river had fallen every hour.

I had just returned home from school when we heard Jossie Hyatt calling for help from across the river. The *Water Queen* Showboat had settled down on a ledge and was tipping over sideways into the river at the landing. Dad, Tommy, and our cousins Frank and Billy Reynolds, rushed to her aid, but to no avail. They only had time to throw off a few pieces of furniture and disconnect the *Ida Mae* from the stern of the showboat. Then they forcefully carried Jossie, kicking and screaming, to safety just as the *Water Queen's* superstructure slid off the hull into the river. It was carried to its final destination on the Ohio River. Thus ended the illustrious career of the *Water Queen* Showboat.

With Roy Hyatt confined to a lung treatment center in North Carolina, Jossie had been alone on her beloved showboat. Like a sea captain going down with his ship, she wanted to stay with the showboat to the end. She was heart broken. You could hear her crying all over the waterfront. Though we invited her to stay with us until Roy could be with her again, she retired to their home at Lowel, Ohio.

Our roster this year was Jack Griffeth, the director and characters; Margaret Williams Griffeth (who was disowned by her family when she married and went into show business), and Vernon Smoot. They were all carryovers from he *Water Queen* Showboat. Newcomers were Owen Miller, Harold and Wava Blodgett; Ernie and Jeanie St. Clair who previously toured with us; and Hap Moore was back for his sixth season.

"Flower of the Rancho," a four act western drama, plus five vaudeville acts were the opening bill at Point Pleasant April 10, 1936.

I starred in the leading role of Roxy, and Harold Blodgett had the co-starring part. The supporting cast included my sister, Margaret, in her first ingenue part; Tommy, Frank, and Owen Miller had bit parts; and our German shepherd, Pal, starred in the role of a "killer dog," with me as his trainer.

Owen Miller and Tommy kept a constant flow of piano and drum music coming from the pit during intermission and the prize candy sale, then opened the vaudeville revue with "Waiting for the Robert E. Lee."

The acts, introduced by Jack Griffeth, were Wava Blodgett and Company, five yellow ducks doing cute tricks were the company; Wiggles and Giggles, an adagio dance by Ernie and Jeanie St. Clair; stand-up comedian, singing and dancing by Hap Moore; a comedy bit, "The Country Bumkin" by Jack and Margaret Griffeth; and a brother and sister dance team, Tommy and Margaret Reynolds. Tommy's comical monkey walk and Russian dancing always stopped the show.

It wasn't long until I took over Owen Miller's job on the piano and calliope. He was a very likeable man and a fine musician. Dad hated to let him go, but he was hitting the bottle too much and it interfered with his work. Drink seemed to be the curse of piano and calliope players.

After playing the 7:30 calliope concert I hurried to the front of the showboat to help Margaret sell popcorn. She nudged me and said, "Look over there." It was a fishing line being dangled over the side of the boat from the upper deck. Margaret hung a bagful of popcorn on it and giving the line a jerk, up it went, followed by mischievous giggling. It wasn't long until the line appeared again and Margaret put another bagful on the hook. It was our little brothers, Jack and John. Garnett had left them in bed asleep when she came downstairs to sell tickets. They were just pretending to be asleep and got away with it every night. "They're the cutest things I ever saw," Margaret commented.

Dropping everything at the sound of the whistle signal, I returned to the calliope playing, "Down by the Old Mill Stream, By the Light of the Silvery Moon, Let Me Call You Sweetheart, Happy Days Are Here Again, Down By the Riverside," and Dad's favorite, "Maggie."

Back and forth I went selling popcorn and playing the calliope. At 8:30 sharp, Tommy, Margaret, saxophonist, and I moved into the orchestra pit and opened the show with the "12 Street Rag, The Beer Barrel Polka," and "The Tiger Rag."

Then we left the pit, running to take our places on stage. There we became three different characters in the play *"Flower of the Rancho."* Tommy and I also kept a constant flow of music going during intermission and the candy sale. I soloed the vaudeville revue and finale, and played "Good Night Sweetheart," on the piano and led the singing until everybody left the theatre.

Dad proudly told us, "I get a lot of compliments about the show and the good work you kids are doing. A number of people have told me it's worth the price of admission just to watch Tommy play the drums."

Our alternate presentation was *"Hillbilly Detective,"* with a change of vaudeville acts.

On our way back down the Ohio, *"Dolly of the Follies,"* was our next play along with new vaudeville revue. I was cast in the title role of Dolly. During rehearsals I had trouble with my French accent. Finally, director Griffeth threw up his hands in frustration, dramatically looked heavenward and said, "Oh, God, please send me an actress who can speak French!"

It was hilarious. I laughed and laughed, but the next time I did it right.

> *Billboard* – July 15, 1936 – "Hap Moore, back on the *Majestic* Showboat this season postcards that the T. J. Reynolds floating theatre is enjoying good business to date. Members of the cast tendered a surprise birthday party in the showboat dining room to Mrs. T. J. Reynolds, June 18. There were lots of ice cream and cake, followed by dancing and the outfit." Moore reports, "Didn't get to bed until 12 o'clock, by gosh! We're like a big family on here. Life is just one town after the other. We go to bed at one night stand and wake up in the next."

After a seven year run in Pittsburgh, Captain Menke signed on a Major Bowes Amateur unit to tour with the *Goldenrod* Showboat. Charging 50¢ admission, they presented matinee and evening performances along the Ohio River.

One day, when they were playing nearby, Margaret, Anna, and I rowed upriver to see a matinee. The *Goldenrod* was in poor condition. I couldn't believe how much it had deteriorated. The once beautiful red velvet upholstered seats were threadbare and pulling apart at the seams. We had to watch where we stepped to keep from going through the rotted floorboards. But when that lively bunch of entertainers came on stage the shabbiness was forgotten. It was a good show and we enjoyed our time aboard the grand old showboat.

We spent most of our free time shopping uptown or playing in the river. If we weren't rowing in the skiff and diving into the waves left in the wake of passing steamboats, we were diving and swimming off the side deck of the *Atta Boy*, or walking the paddle wheel and diving off it.

I don't know who thought of it first, but Tommy and Frank tied their dirty overalls on the paddle wheel before making the jump to the next town. By the time we arrived they were spotlessly clean. They had to gauge the distance, like an automatic timer on a washing machine, or there wouldn't be anything left of them.

One day, when I was alone in swimming, I took my first high dive off the top deck of the *Atta Boy* and ended up underneath the boat, and couldn't find my way back out. I continued to run my hand along the snake infested, moss covered bottom of the hull as I propelled myself along feeling one way and then the other for a way out. I didn't know which way to turn and the longer I struggled the weaker I became. Then I felt it – the edge of the boat, and out I came desperately gasping for air. I could've drowned and Dad wouldn't have known what became of me.

Following a trip on the Tennessee River I began having chills, fever, and night sweats. One morning coming into the landing at Rising Sun, Indiana, I stopped in the middle of a calliope concert, made my way below deck and collapsed.

I woke up in my own bed. Dad and Garnett had been keeping watch over me. I had been in a coma for three days.

"You've been awfully sick. The doctor said you had malaria fever and for me to give you quinine tablets and whiskey. I told him I'd give you the quinine, but not the whiskey," Dad emphasized.

The show went on as scheduled during my absence, but without the piano and calliope. I was the only one on board who could play them. Tommy and Margaret provided saxophone and drum music in the pit. Instead of *"Flower of the Rancho,"* a full-length variety show with plenty of singing, dancing, magic, comedy, skits and bits were presented.

We made one day layover to visit Aunt Ida and Uncle Tegie at New Port, Kentucky, when we passed Cincinnati. They now owned a house on Park Street near the waterfront. Aunt Ida was still raising and selling canaries and Uncle Tegie was betting on horses.

I loved Cincinnati. Aunt Ida, Margaret, and I had a wonderful time shopping in the department stores. I bought a snazzy three quarter length leopard coat and matching stovepipe hat.

The excursion steamer *Island Queen* was shuttling passengers to Coney Island, and the *Bryant's* Showboat was playing at the foot of Lawrence Street. In the evening both their calliopes could be heard. Billy Bryant's lovely wife, Josephine, was their calliopist. "Tiptoe Through the Tulips," was her trademark.

That evening I rowed Aunt Ida, Margaret and myself across the river to the *Bryant's* Showboat to see the show. We were met by Billy Bryant and chatted for a while. Then we went to the front of the showboat where Josephine was at the window selling tickets. "Go on in, be our guests," she said, refusing our money. We found seats to our liking along the balcony wing. A near capacity crowd was on board for the show.

Billy Bryant introduced all the dignitaries in the audience and had them stand up and take a bow. I was taken by surprise when he said, "Ladies and gentlemen, I want you to meet a very special guest, the leading lady, piano and calliope player for the *Majestic* Showboat . . . Captain Reynold's lovely daughter, Catherine!"

Josephine Bryant played several selections on the piano. Then the show got underway with the three generations of Bryants and two other actors making up the cast. *"Tess of the Rockies,"* a three act drama featured Betty Bryant in the title role. Betty was a little younger than me, an only child, and cute as could be. She was also very talented.

Four vaudeville specialties sandwiched in between the acts of the play were presented. They included a solo, "When Ma was Courting Pa," and eccentric dance by Betty Bryant; a monologue and tap dance while sitting on a chair by Billy Bryant; a magic Act by the elder Samuel Bryant; a song parody, "Sucking Cider Through A Straw" by another comic; followed by an old-time Sing-Along with illustrated slides flashed on the screen. The handsome leading man sang "Let A Smile Be Your Umbrella," and ended the show.

At Boncar, W. Va., head of the Great Kanawha River, I played the songs, "The West Virginia Hills," "Listen to the Mockingbird" in stop-time duet with the mountain echo for variation on the calliope. At the end of a musical phrase I'd wait until the tootling whistles refrain resounded from hill to hill along the river, then played the next one, etc. It was very pleasing to the listeners, especially Dad who requested it.

On our return trip downriver we included an Amateur Contest in the vaudeville revue. All the towns had their share of talented singers, dancers, musicians and comics of all ages who came down to the boat during the day to audition for the contest. I accompanied them at the piano.

The ones receiving the loudest and prolonged applause were the winners. The third runner-up received 50¢; the second runner-up $1; the first runner-up $1.50; and the big winner got $2. But their biggest prize was performing on the *Majestic's* stage in front of their home-town folks and families.

Chapter 13
The Great Flood

January, 1937, floodwaters from the Ohio and Kanawha Rivers, and Old Town and Crooked Creek, inundated Point Pleasant and Henderson, West Virginia.

An emergency was declared. Working in conjunction with the Red Cross, the Point Pleasant Flood Commission set up kitchens and shelters to aid the flood victims. The National Guard, Coast Guard, WPA, and volunteer workers were called out to help. Row boats replaced cars and trucks on the streets evacuating people and household belongings to shelters. Some were taken by school buses to the National Reserves at Camp Conley, north of town. People had to be helped out of upper story windows into boats, and off rooftops of houses floating off their foundations in the floodwaters. Sightseers were warned to stay off the streets with their boats or face a stiff fine.

Meanwhile, the *Majestic* was setting high and dry in the treetops at her landing. She served as an emergency aid station for our side of the river. The workers and their families came by the boatloads to get hot vegetable soup, coffee, sandwiches, and milk given out by Dad and me from the lower front deck of the showboat. First aid was administered by Garnett. She also made hundreds of cookies and doughnuts. We distributed boots, warm clothing and blankets provided by the Flood Commission.

In addition, the *Majestic* was loaded with furniture, personal belongings, dogs, cats, and refugees. My sister, Hazel, Charley and their three sons, Charles, Jr., George Norman, and Thomas Jefferson Bates, were among the first residents to be run out of their waterfront home by the flood.

February 11, 1937, a flood stage of 62.9 feet was recorded at Point Pleasant, on level with the terrible flood of 1913. But a lot of river people, including Dad, didn't agree with that figure, saying it was much higher. Most of Point Pleasant was under water, as were every town and village along the Ohio and its tributaries.

Thousands of people fled their homes and businesses when the Ohio poured over weakened flood walls and levees into the towns. Bridges crumbled, sections of roadways and waterfront properties were washed away. Trains carrying refugees were washed off the tracks, and automobiles off the roads. Buildings were swept off their foundations and crushed against one another. Towns were left in shambles or completely swept away by the raging floodwaters. L⁻ ⁻es were lost and property damage was estimated to be in the millions ⌐ dollars in at least eight states as a result of the flood, the worst in the century.

By the first of April the water had receded, the boats were shipshape, actors on board, and rehearsals over. With the calliope playing "Here Comes the Showboat," we opened the season at the foot of our landing in Henderson. We had a full house, including two talent scouts from Warner Brothers Motion Picture Studio in California.

I had the title role in *"Diane's Atonement,"* and sang "She May Be Somebody's Baby," with recitation, in the vaudeville revue.

Other specialties were a comedy bit by Jack and Margaret Griffeth; a song duet by Earl and his new wife Jean Whittaker; buck and wing dancing by Toby Veva and Hap Moore; Conversation with Polly Parrot and song "I'm a Hot Petunia," by Harry Clark; and Russian and tap dancing by Tommy and Margaret Reynolds.

After the show Dad told me, "The talent scouts from Warner Brothers wanted to give you a screen test. I asked them where you'd have to go for the screen test, and they said California. So I told them to forget it. You're my star performer and I need you. You have your work cut out for you here."

With Earl Whittaker at the calliope playing "River Stay Away From My Door," we began wending our way up the Kanawha. We passed *Bryant's* Showboat lying at the city wharf at Charleston, W. Va. After leaving Henderson they had worked their way there, then back to Cincinnati for the summer.

With the Menke Brothers *Hollywood* Showboat playing towns along the Mississippi River, and the *Goldenrod* going into permanent stock at St. Louis, Mo., the *Majestic* was still the only showboat in operation on the Ohio River and its tributaries.

Parkersburg News – May 14, 1937 – "Showboat opened engagement here. Offering *"Clouds and Sunshine,"* a four act comedy (endorsed as a great moral lesson), and

vaudeville revue of six acts, the *Majestic* Showboat, owned
and operated by T. J. Reynolds, opened in Parkersburg for
an indefinite engagement. Eleven persons are in the cast.
Seats are on sale during the day at the boat, tied up near the
mouth of the Little Kanawha River."

Parkersburg News – May 16 – *Majestic* Pleases Audience. A near capacity crowd attended the showboat
Majestic last night. The play *"Clouds and Sunshine,"*
gleaned a lot of applause and laughter.

The *Majestic* players are proving more and more
popular with each performance and if present indications
are any criteria, the boat is due for an extended stay.

In the vaudeville revue last night Margaret Reynolds
completely stopped the show with a neatly executed tap
dance. The audience would not permit another act to go
on, until Miss Reynolds accepted an encore, which she
gracefully complied with.

For tonight, *"Why Lindy Ran Away,"* a three act
comedy drama, featuring Margaret Reynolds in the title
role, will be presented as a change of play and will run
through Tuesday."

While at Parkersburg Margaret, Ruth, Agnes Clark, and I had
a wonderful time browsing through the five and dime and department stores. We also went to the Hagenback Wallas Circus featuring
Tom Mix and his trained horse.

East Liverpool, Ohio, "Over The Waves With Miss Fisher
– Most of us have read it, or seen it on the screen, or
listened to its tunes. The roll of "Ol' Man River." Ameri-
cans have come to think of "Showboat" as a legend, a
grand old tale that isn't true anymore, but it is.

Today I saw it come true, through a lucky break and
a captain's kind heart. What a day.

The *Majestic* alone makes its yearly pilgrimage up
past Pittsburgh and back, April to October.

Eleven actors present this season's repertoire; *"Clouds
and Sunshine, Diane's Atonement, The Marriage of Elizabeth."*
Sunday night I went to learn *"Why Lindy Ran Away."*

The calliope, atop the tow boat, *Atta Boy* tootled "Beautiful Ohio" and "Over the Waves." Down the wharf came the
last nighters, strolling, some carrying babies, some with
canes.

I sat with my bag of popcorn, watching the auditorium fill. The river breeze blew in from the open door, and out in the dusk launch lights went by, followed by waves that teetered the auditorium and made us squeal.

The piano and drums overture struck up with a whirl. Bulbs blinked out, and the curtain rolled high, revealing the first scene.

The captain's nine sons and daughters were all born on showboats. Two are married; the rest are with him now. Catherine, 18, and Margaret, 13, have sister acts; they also take parts in the play; help sell popcorn and novelties, and play the piano. Catherine practices the calliope. When she was a beginner, she tells us, Daddy used to take the boat to some lonely stretch in the river then I'd play."

Ever think of the problem of practicing an instrument that can be heard 10 miles when the wind is right? I wanted to try the calliope.

We were in no lonely stretch, but docked at Shippingport. With my fading piano technique to guide me, I tried to pounce on some chords. The keyboard looked the same, but there was something vitally different. Where Mr. Whittaker drew sweet pipings, I drew tortured squawks that could be heard for 10 miles.

You must press the keys all the way down, I learned and release them after just the right interval, else too little or too much steam blows out of the pipes. Catherine's fingers sprain easily when she's out of practice.

"It's a lazy life on the river," smiles one lady of the cast. She strolled on deck, her green parrot on her finger, to watch us go through the lock at Midland. She explains that troupers usually sleep late mornings, after the night shows."

What happens in this lazy, but lonely life. The tempo of things is slowed, as we moved upriver between blue green hills, round gentle bends, 10 miles, maybe 20 or 30 miles a day . . . stories swapped in the pilothouse . . . Catherine sewing sunsuits for her little nephews . . . Mrs. Reynolds hemming sheets for the showboat family . . . Bill and Tommy uncoiling rope, recoiling it more neatly . . . Pal, the affectionate German Police, reigning on the top deck . . . Children run down the bank and shout "Stop here! Come on in here!" they plead.

We dock. Maybe some of us go to explore the village. Some boys start off leisurely with handbills. Mr. Whitaker comes on board with a bouquet of roses and lemon lilies, the gift of friends with a garden up the bank. There are friends all along the way. They watch for the showboat every year. Sometimes life isn't so lazy, when there is a new play, there's rehearsals. And last summer, that tornado, young Catherine had to get out and help handle the boat. The wind makes the big boat just like a sail, only you can't take in the sail.

Many a fresh sunny morning will find me thinking of the river. I'll shut my eyes and be standing behind the calliope again. "Here Comes the Showboat."

Pal is cavorting on the top deck, children are waving and dancing at the water edge. Underneath, the *Atta Boy* is chugging happily.

"Here comes the sho-ow boat."

The captain bends the wheel, the dock comes nearer, the wind races through our hair. All our flags are flying. "Here comes the showboat."

Out of the blue, the Whittakers gave notice and left the boat with their four-year-old daughter Barbra Ann. So I went back to playing the piano and calliope full time. Steve and Grace DeVeres were hired in their place. They were former players with the *Majestic* in the early 20's. Steve was a fine saxophone player and joined Tommy, Margaret and me in the pit.

Toby was the first person up the hill at the towns every morning to get the mail. "Oh, look, Catherine got another letter from Harry," he'd say, and teasingly held it up for everybody to see. One day I showed one of my letters and a picture of Harry to Anna.

"Are you going to answer it, and thank him for the picture?" she asked.

"Maybe," I replied. I seldom answered any of his letters.

"Shame on you! Harry's a fine young man. It would not hurt you to sit down and write him a few lines," she scolded.

I did, and the letters kept coming and I kept answering them. One day, to my surprise, a hundred miles from nowhere, here came Harry and a buddy to see me. He was the last person I expected to see. We laughed and talked for awhile and I asked them to stay for supper.

Harry said he couldn't stay because his mom didn't know where he was. They were visiting relatives and he had to get back before she missed him.

Everywhere we traveled that summer we were saddened to see the destruction the flood had caused. Familiar landscapes had undergone drastic changes. Work crews were cleaning up the wreckage, repairing roads, bridges, and rebuilding towns back from the river.

At Cairo, Illinois, the 60-foot floodwall protecting the town from floodwaters off the Ohio and Upper Mississippi River was all that kept it from being swept away. After the flood large locks with roller dams to control the river were built, as were floodwalls in many towns, including Point Pleasant.

Harry was standing at the top of the hill waving to me when we pulled into the city wharf at Point Pleasant. I saw him again that evening when he came to the show. He sat in the balcony watching me perform. After the show he asked me to go uptown with him for a bite to eat at Vicker's Restaurant.

Then we walked arm and arm in the moonlight. All the attraction we had for one another since childhood came rushing back. Before leaving me at the head of the gangplank, he gave me a note saying, "I wrote this for you." It was a poem titled – "My Little Redhead"

The showboat lands with all the noise
That fascinates the girls and boys,
But the way it affects me, I stand apart,
It doesn't mean fun . . . it means my heart.
My heart had returned, it has come back to me,
In the shape of a girl. There she is! Now I see!
Her hair is red, she is freckle face,
No other girl can take her place.
But now she is here, and my heart is gay,
It will be . . . until she goes away.

Chapter 14
Courtship and Marriage

At Point Pleasant High School I received double credits and a "B" average in my catch-up work. I was also taking piano lessons from Florence Arnet, a former teacher, who gave me my high school equivalent test.

One day that winter, Ruth came home from school, reached out to Dad, and fainted. He rushed her to the hospital where the diagnosis was meningitis. She was in and out of the hospital and it took many months of physical therapy for her to regain her strength. We all pulled together as a family and helped entertain and take care of her. But in time, she overcame her illness and was able to go back to school and resume her life as usual.

On weekends I worked in Women's Wear at Morrison's Department Store. I went with Harry to Sunday evening services at the Southern Methodist Church and movies at the Alpine Theatre.

Harry played guitar, mandolin, banjo, and harmonica with a local band. Bum Miller, Elmer McDermitt, Tracy Simpkins and Harry were the "Midnight Ramblers." They played for youth groups, lodges, parties, and made guest appearances over WCHS Radio Station in Charleston, West Virginia. Harry was working as a salesman at Harper's Furniture Store. After work he walked me home across the Shadle Bridge, spanning the Kanawha River.

He continued to write more poems expressing thoughts he was too shy to say in person. It wasn't long until I had a notebook full of them. Dad read all of them and knew how serious we were getting. His only comment was, "Harry's a pretty good poet. You should set some of his poems to music."

One night when we were slowly walking arm and arm across the bridge in the moonlight, he stopped midway, and taking me in his arms, asked me to marry him.

Thinking he was a lot like my father and that he was the right one for me, I said, "Yes, but you'll have to ask Dad first."

At the boat Harry walked right up to Dad and said, "Mr. Reynolds, I love Catherine and would like to have your permission to marry her."

After a long silence, Garnett asked me, "Do you love Harry, and want to marry him?"

"Yes," I said.

Getting up from his rocking chair, Dad shook Harry's hand and told him, "It's all right with me, if that's what Catherine wants." And went on to say, "I like you, Harry, and think you and Catherine will make a fine pair. But instead of you taking her away from us and show business, I'd like for you to join us. Think about it, I'd make it worth your while."

Harry whisked me into the kitchen, where he slipped a diamond engagement ring on my finger. Then we kissed. Hearing giggling we turned around and there were Dad, Garnett, Margaret, Ruth, Jack, John, and Roy peeking around the door watching and laughing.

It was also my 19th birthday and Harry gave me a gold wrist-watch to match my ring. Garnett had baked me a cake, so we had a double celebration. The Kings also celebrated our engagement at their home.

We planned to marry in the fall, following our next tour. But after the actors arrived and rehearsals of the drama, *"The Girl and the Game,"* got underway with me cast in the leading role of Nellie Mayo, we decided not to wait and get married during the opening of the show.

In addition to myself, the dramatic cast included Harry Rollins, George B. Hill, Ernest "Toby" Veva, Fred Campbell, Mary Wagner, and Helene Hill.

A capacity crowd of enthusiastic showboatgoers turned out at Gallipolis, Monday night, April 15, for the performance. Paul and Tommy got the show off to a good start with their piano and drum overture. Margaret and I, in blue spangled gowns, opened the vaudeville revue with a duet "College Rhythm" and tap dance. It was followed by George and Helene Hill with a slapstick comedy bit; Jack and Margaret Griffeth, a comedy bit; a baritone solo and dramatization of "When You and I Were Young, Maggie" by Harry and Mary Rollins; a song parody and eccentric dancing by Toby Veva; and Tommy with his showstopper Russian Dance.

In his closing announcement Jack Griffeth invited everybody to attend our wedding at the Presbyterian Church following the show.

I quickly removed my makeup, put on my wedding dress, and pinned Harry's Lily of the Valley corsage on my shoulder. Then, putting on the blue garter Helene Hill had given me to wear for good luck, and carrying the white lace handkerchief Mary Rollins loaned me for something borrowed, I went with the family and actors to the church.

The church was decorated with lighted candles, flowers, and potted palm trees. It was filled with fans from the showboat, close friends, relatives and newspaper reporters.

Harry looked handsome in his powder blue suit. The pipe organ sounded strains of "Here Comes the Bride."

Harry's sister, Wilma, was my matron of honor and her husband, Marcus McDaniel, his best man.

Reverend Gishler addressed the wedding party, then we solemnly repeated our vows. Harry slipped the wedding band on my finger, and we were pronounced man and wife.

We honeymooned aboard the boat until the change of program. Then with Harry wanting me all to himself for awhile, I bid good-by to my family and the life I loved on the river and we left to take up housekeeping in our new home in Bellemeade, three miles north of Point Pleasant.

It would be awhile before the utility companies ran their lines our way. But, I was used to carrying water, doing laundry on the board, and not having indoor plumbing. Like everybody else in the neighborhood, we also had a little house behind the big house, and a coal shed.

With the nation still recovering from the depression, foodstuff was cheap. Our groceries cost only $2.95 a week and lamp oil was 5¢ a week. We bought non-perishable items and smoked meat in large quantities. So even though Harry only made ten dollars a week, we still saved money. I was right at home knowing how to manage.

We soon had our little bungalow looking like a picture in *Good Housekeeping*. There was just one thing wrong with it, I couldn't see the river and boats going by, but we could hear their whistles. I couldn't run out the door and dive into the river when I wanted to swim.

Living on land was a whole new world to me. I had to get used to staying in one place, and getting the feel of mother earth under my feet. I also had to remember not to throw garbage out the back door. The river wasn't there to carry it away. I was like a fish out of water.

My cousin, Frank Reynolds, married Harry's niece Catherine Mae King, and bought a house across the street from us. So we had some company.

It wasn't long until I began feeling seasick and the boat wasn't rocking. I craved dill pickles in the wee hours of the morning. Harry hoped it would be a son, I wanted a daughter. I spent many happy hours making baby dresses, knitting sweaters, caps, shawls, and crib blankets.

When the showboat appeared at Gallipolis on its way upbound on the Ohio, I was so anxious to see the family that we beat the boat coming in. The calliope could be heard resounding along the river. The sound of the music and the sight of the showboat gliding over the water, with Dad at the wheel, was so beautiful I couldn't hold back the tears.

I gave Dad a big hug as he met us coming up the gangplank. Grinning broadly, he said, "It's good to see you. We've missed you. It's not the same with you gone. Not a day goes by without us missing you. The people want to know what became of you? You have a lot of friends along the river, more than you know."

When the boat came in for the winter Dad rowed me across the river to visit. I never missed a Saturday going to the boat. It was like old times housed up in the family quarters watching the kids play.

December 22nd, I went to help Garnett with her Christmas shopping, and ended up staying two weeks. Going up the back stairway with a load of packages I tripped and fell backwards down the steep steps onto the deck below. My baby wasn't due yet, but I began having symptoms.

Garnett talked with my doctor, then called Harry at work. She told him to come to the boat, that we'd be staying for awhile. Shortly after midnight, December 24, I went into labor. Dad insisted on rushing me by boat to the hospital, but I refused because I wanted to have my baby on the showboat the way my Mother and Garnett had their children.

Garnett took over, calling the doctor and making all the preparations for the delivery. Harry built up the fire in the small coal stove. We were in the stateroom of our old family apartment on the back deck of the showboat.

The hours slipped slowly by with Garnett and Harry by my side and Dad checking on me throughout the night. As the sun was peeking over the horizon, I gave birth to a beautiful girl. What a thrill it was to hear her first cry and hold her in my arms. She was the best Christmas present I could have wished for.

We named her Margaret Catherine. Margaret for my mother and sister, and Catherine for both myself and Harry's mother. Margaret Catherine was the only grandchild born aboard the *Majestic,* and destined to be our only child.

Garnett insisted that I stay in bed and rest until the ninth day. Quoting an old midwife's tale, "It's so your organs will go back in place and you won't have trouble afterwards," she said.

When Harry and I returned home with the baby there was a big upright player piano setting in our living room. He'd bought it from Velora Shiveron, in Henderson, for $25. She was tired of moving it every time there was a flood.

A few months later we got a telegram with bus fare from Dad saying, "Join boat tomorrow at Leavenworth, Ind. Need piano and calliope player."

"Do you want to go?" Harry asked.

"Yes," I replied. "I can't turn Dad down. He needs me."

Mrs. Lulla Harper, Harry's employer, gave him a leave of absence and promised his job would be waiting when he returned in the fall. Then the following morning, with Catherine Mae giving us a farewell breakfast, we boarded a Greyhound bus with Margaret Catherine and all the luggage we could carry, and headed for the showboat.

We had one changeover to make at Louisville, Ky., but found there were no other buses scheduled to leave that evening. It was after six o'clock and we had over fifty miles to go over unpaved river roads to Leavenworth. A young man finally agreed to take us there in his beat-up Model T Ford for $25. We piled into the car and tried to make it to the showboat before show time.

Dad was waiting on the front of the boat, grinning from ear to ear. Shaking Harry's hand, he told him, "Boy, am I glad to see you and Catherine and little Margaret. I was beginning to think you weren't coming. I've got a big crowd on board. It's almost show time, and no one to play the piano."

Taking Margaret Catherine from my arms, Garnett told me, "Don't worry," your dad and I will take good care of her while you're working."

Hurrying backstage, Harry got his banjo out of the case, and we went with Margaret and Tommy to play the overture. Once again, I gave the downbeat and we swung out with the "12th Street Rag," and followed with the "Maple Leaf Rag," and "The Tiger Rag." It was like old times. Harry was just what we needed, a good banjo player .

Then due to the absence of the leading man, a full-length vaudeville revue was presented instead of the regularly scheduled program.

The acts and players were "The Country Bumpkin" by Jack and Margaret Griffeth; Singing and dancing by Lanya Young; Woman Impersonator, Harold Lowe; Comedy, singing and dancing, Ron Marlo; tap dance, Miss Margaret Reynolds; Novelty number, playing guitar and harmonica at the same time, Harry King; Pantominist, Philip Pine (who later became a movie actor); singing, Harry Weatherby; monologue and Russian dancing, Thomas Reynolds;

Ventriloquist, Ralph Young; ballet dance, Madeline Pine; magical comedy, Harold Lowe and Tommy Reynolds.

Harold, the magician, draped a white sheet over Tommy. Speaking mumbo jumbo he hypnotized him into leaning back with his feet rising off the floor until he was suspended in the air. Scratching his head he said, "Now, what am I supposed to do? I forgot. I guess I'll just have to leave him there," . . . and left the stage.

"Oh, no you're not!" Tommy said. Throwing off the sheet, he walked offstage carrying the extra legs he had been holding up in front of him.

After the show, Tommy told Harry and me this story. "This morning, after we pulled into the landing without the calliope player, a man on the riverbank asked me "What's the matter, Tommy, don't you have a calliope player on the boat?"

"Not now, but we've got one coming this evening. The best doggonned calliope player on the river!" I told him.

"Come calliope time, there he was, waiting on the riverbank next to the *Atta Boy,* where he could see and listen to you play. Time slipped by and before long a crowd of people were waiting with him. The later it got, the more disappointed Pop looked sitting on the checkpost watching for you and Harry to show up. Finally, I said, "How about me going up there and playing them a little tune on the calliope?"

Pop gave me a funny look, and said, "I didn't know you could play the calliope."

"I can play "Black-eyed Susan Brown" on the piano with two fingers," I told him.

When he quit laughing, he told me, "Go ahead, I'd like to hear that myself!"

"So I went up to the calliope and tried playing the song through a couple of times. It sounded awful!" Like a bunch of dying cows, and the man on the riverbank was fit to be tied," he said. "When I quit playing, he cupped his hands to his mouth and shouted up to me, 'If I had a gun, I'd shoot you!!!' "

Mr. Griffeth gave Harry and me the leading parts in *"Honest Sinners and Saintly Hypocrites,"* and told us, "I thought you might want to look these over tonight and know your lines tomorrow night so we can go back to playing our regular show.

Though it wasn't unusual for me to learn a part to a play in that short time, it was a new experience for Harry. But, with a couple of business rehearsals, the following evening he went on stage and performed like a veteran trouper. He not only won the hearts of the audience with his portrayal of the preacher, he held his cool when a windstorm came up and threatened to blow us loose from the landing during the performance.

We were lying at the desolate landing at Wolf Creek, Kentucky, where the Ohio is a mile wide. Hearing tornado like wind pounding against the side of the showboat and the jerking at her moorings was enough to make anyone run scared. Harry just raised his voice like the rest of us to be heard above the noise and continued acting as if nothing was happening. Since we showed no cause for alarm, the audience calmly remained in their seats watching the show.

We had left Margaret Catherine asleep in our room. Afraid I couldn't get to her in an emergency, I ran upstairs between scenes to bring her backstage. Coming back with her in my arms I was lifted off my feet by the wind. Dad was on the guard, reached out and grabbed hold of us, and kept us from being blown overboard.

As always in times like this, the excitement of the moment was'nt without a bit of humor. The young greenhorn Dad hired to help with the decking was last seen running up the hill.

Harry was a wonderful father. He played with Margaret Catherine and looked after her while I worked. She had no trouble adapting to our schedule. She took a late morning nap and stayed awake the rest of the day so she would sleep while the show was going on in the evening. She was so tired she fell asleep with me sitting on deck rocking, nursing, and singing to her. During the show Harry and I both made trips to check on her. If she did wake up, Ruth, Jack and John kept her entertained until we could take over.

One evening she was fretful because of the extreme heat and nothing would pacify her. So, I brought her backstage and put her on a blanket in the middle of the floor. Then I called Pal, set him down beside her, and placing one of his big paws on her tummy, told him to watch her. Every time we checked on her, Pal was faithfully doing his job, while Margaret Catherine was laughing and enjoying every minute of it.

She loved it when we went swimming. Harry let her float with the support of his hand under her tummy, and one day, to our surprise, she kept right on going and was swimming before she could walk.

It wasn't long until Harry was driving the advance car and helping Tommy with the billing. Ray Lambert, a well-known advance agent for other showboats during their heyday, was hired for the job. But, Dad thought his expense account was too high and let him go.

Ray lived at Cave In Rock, Illinois, where he and his wife owned and operated a restaurant. When we stopped there they gave us a dinner party after the show. Before leaving, Dad left enough money under his plate to more than pay for the nice chicken dinner.

Playing to packed houses and turning people away, we soon arrived at Pittsburgh Landing, Tennessee. Much of the natural beauty of the Tennessee River that we knew and loved was being lost in the way of progress. The TWA built a series of locks and dams flooding the farms and towns that had been there for generations, forming a series of lakes.

We presented *"Honest Sinners and Saintly Hypocrites,"* and the alternate bill was *"The Push."* Harry and I performed a "School Daze" bit and ended the performance with "Whispering" and "Alabama Bound," with Harry on banjo and me accompanying him on the piano.

That summer the *Majestic* was the only showboat still making one night stands. The *Majestic* was fast becoming a relic of the past, as was the familiar strains of her calliope. Dad always said, "People didn't stop coming to the showboats, showboats stopped going to the people." So he intended to keep going and bring entertainment to the "willows" and cities for as long as he was able, and had his family to help him."

The show was brought to a close at Manchester, Ohio in late October. As we were leaving the boat to return to our home, Dad told Harry, "You and Catherine make an unbeatable showboat team. I wish you'd stay in the business."

Although it was wonderful making the tour aboard the showboat with Harry and Margaret Catherine, it was also nice to be back in our home again for the winter.

Chapter 15
New Life for the
Majestic and *Atta Boy*

That winter Dad performed the most outstanding carpentry feat of his career. The *Majestic* and *Atta Boy* both needed new hulls at the close of the season. To avoid the high cost of having the work done at the Marietta Shipyards at Point Pleasant, he devised a unique plan so he could do all the work himself at his landing.

He ordered the lumber he would need from a mill in Oregon, home of the mammoth Douglas Fir trees. There were timbers for the gunnels measuring 190 feet in length, bottom planks 3 by 12 by 28 feet long, etc. The lumber was shipped by flatcars to Henderson. It was then pulled by work mules to our landing, where it was stacked in neat piles waiting for Dad to bring the boats in for the winter.

With Tommy, Revena King (Harry's older brother), Wes Sealy, his carpenter helpers, Charles and Charles Sullivan, Jr., laborers, they built the new hull for the *Majestic* on the riverbank by the boat.

A runway of tree branches stripped of bark and lubricated with axle grease was built. They moved the showboat up shore out of the way, started the engine aboard the *Atta Boy* and pulled the new hull off the stocks down the runway into the river.

The hull, which would serve a twofold purpose before putting it on the showboat, was readied for sinking. They built scaffolds along the topsides of the gunnels and placed a water drum on each one, bored two 4-inch holes above the waterline, and left the hull overnight to sink. Next morning only an inch of water had come into the hull. They dumped a load of heavy chains and wire cables into the hull to weight it down. This, along with water pumped into the drums made the hull sink out of sight. The top half of the drums were visible above the surface of the water.

Henderson residents gathered on the bank watching. Other carpenters, who kept daily watch warned, "Tom, she's a goner." Boat builders he'd discussed his plan with told him he was taking a chance in losing his boats.

Now that the hull was sunk, the trick was to use it as a dry dock for the *Atta Boy*. The towboat was floated over the submerged hull between the scaffolds and water drums.Then as the drums were pumped dry, the hull slowly resurfaced, lifting the *Atta Boy* out of the water on the temples. The holes were plugged and the remaining water siphoned out of the hull, making it a dry roomy place for them to work. In less than two weeks they had the old hull torn off and a new one built on the *Atta Boy*.

One evening Dad told Tommy, "Let's sink the hull, move the towboat off and put the *Majestic* on it. The carpenters will be surprised when they come to work in the morning."

They moved the *Atta Boy* out of the way and pulled the showboat, by ropes, into position over the submerged hull. It was a crucial time. Everything had to be perfect to make it work.

The water pumps were started, draining the water from the drums. Time ticked by. Finally, the hull rose up around the bottom of the showboat, and stopped short of the mark. "It's not going to work. Let's plug up the holes and fill up the drums again. We're going to have to saw those damn rake planks off. They're binding the hull on each end," he told Tommy.

When that was done, they resurfaced the hull again, and it lifted the showboat high and dry out of the river on the cross timbers, just as Dad had envisioned.

Next morning they put eighty screw jacks under the cabin to hold it up. Then they tore out the old hull, substituting the new one as a dry dock. The cabin was lowered eighteen inches onto the new hull. Cabin walls were spread out one foot at the bottom to line up with it. Dad said, "Now the showboat's streamlined, and harder to turn over."

The operation was a complete success. The *Majestic* and *Atta Boy* got their new hulls at a minimum of cost, giving them another lease on life. During the whole operation, only one window was broken. Dad was right. His plan did work. He showed the so-called experts.

Captain Billy Bryant, whose showboat was still in winter harbor at the landing above us, and had watched the entire operation, summed it up. "Tom, I have to hand it to you. Only a genius could accomplish what you just did. It was beau-ti-ful!! Simp-ly, beau-ti-ful!!!!"

Then they set the stage back sixteen feet to enlarge the theatre and increase seating capacity on the main floor and in the balcony, from 425 to 500 people. The only way to go was back, cutting down the size of the backstage area and staterooms upstairs. Dad was lucky finding seats to match. He bought them from Hoff's old Opera House in Point Pleasant.

After he and Tommy slapped on another coat of paint the showboat was ready for another season on the river.

Dad was disappointed when we didn't go out with the boat that spring. But, it wasn't long until Harry took another leave of absence from his work, locked up the house, jumped into our Chevy, and headed for the showboat at Manchester, Ohio.

Catherine Mae, who was joining Frank for a trip on an oil barge, went with us as far as Manchester. Our car ran all right, but the tires were bad. When they got overheated they ballooned out in places like blowing bubble gum. We had to stop and wait for them to cool down before going on our way.

Finally, we made it, with everybody on hand to greet us. "My favorite people! The one family. One man, one woman, and one child. It's good to have you back with us," Jack Griffeth said, pumping Harry's hand.

We settled in our room on the upper back deck of the showboat. Tommy had steam popping in the boiler. So, at the sound of the whistle signal, I went to the calliope and began playing, to let people living several miles from the river know we were there.

"Lure of the City," a comedy drama in three acts, was the current bill. The cast was Jack and Margaret Griffeth, Al and Ruby Audrey, Billy and Beverly Van, Margaret Reynolds, Buster Brandt, and Toby Veva.

For the first time I didn't have a part in the play, but kept busy playing piano and calliope and doing a vaudeville act with Harry. We ended the show with Harry playing a banjo solo, followed by the grand finale, "So Long, We'll See You Again."

We had three cars, our car, the advance car, and Buster Brandt's new red Cadillac Convertible. Our car was one too many. So, we sold it at a profit and Harry went back to driving the advance car and posting bills with Tommy. Jack also helped post bills on occasion and distributed handbills at the towns.

Dad was a happy man. He had all of us kids with him, except Hazel. Marion, who was a widower, was visiting. He had a son, Marion, Jr., who was being raised by his maternal grandmother. Marion loved watermelons, so Dad bought a whole field of them and stored them in the hull, so he could have all he wanted.

It wasn't long until we had so many actors we had a hard time making extra room for them. We took on six tent show performers that had been left stranded at Eddyville, Ky. They were Mr. and Mrs.

Lemmons, Tintype, Daisy Boyington, who was formerly with the Grand Ole Opry, and Bill and Mike.

Though they said they would work for room and board until they could find other employment, Dad put them on the payroll. He liked the idea of having eighteen people in the show, so he kept them on as extras.

They fit right in with our way of life and loved every minute of it. They had no more tents to put up and take down come rain or shine, or packing up and moving on to the next town. On the boat they had more leisure time to sit around and relax, sleep, and enjoy living and traveling on the showboat. The money was sure and we all got along well together.

Mr. Lemmons was a fine pianist and could make the old calliope talk when he alternated playing the concerts with me. His wife, a pretty young redhead, was wardrobe mistress for their tent show.

Though everybody liked him, Tintype was an odd ball. Every morning after arriving in a new town, he'd ask children on the riverbank if any men had died there recently. If they had, he'd ask if they were about his size. If the answer was yes, he'd ask where they'd lived. Then he'd go up town, knock on the widow's door and ask to buy his clothes.

Every now and then we'd see him come back with a nice suit of clothes draped over one arm, shirts, ties, and pants on the other arm. Sometimes he'd be wearing two or more hats on his head and be carrying a pair of dress shoes. He was always well dressed, and had a fine stage wardrobe, and it was obvious where he got them. The clothes he didn't want he sold at a profit after the show closed.

Bill and Mike loved to go in swimming. They virtually lived in the river when we weren't traveling or working. They even rigged up a diving bell out of a 50 pound lard can with an air hose connection, and used a tire pump to generate air while underwater. They tied weights to their ankles and had a wonderful time taking turns pumping air and walking around on the river bottom.

"Ten Nights in a Barroom," was the alternate bill. Jack Griffeth was excellent in his portrayal of the drunkard. Margaret Reynolds was little Mary, who died after reforming her father and went to heaven (into the stage loft by block and tackle). I was the leader of the temperance movement, and Harry was the inn keeper. Everybody was in the play, some at the table playing cards, at the bar drinking, and some with bit parts. Dad asked Ester, Tommy's wife, if she'd like to be in the play, but she just giggled at the thought and shook her head no.

For our vaudeville act, Toby Veva, Harry and I teamed up in a "Ragtime Wedding" bit. Then Harry and I strolled arm in arm and sang "How Would You Like to be a Kid Again," with Mr. Lemmons accompanying us at the piano.

Sometimes while billing, Harry had several hours to wait at the landings before the showboat arrived. Occasionally Margaret Catherine and I went with him in the car. One night lying at a remote landing in Kentucky, Dad told Harry, "I've got a long way to go to the next town. If you don't mind driving the advance car, I'd like to leave tonight. Maybe Catherine would like to go along and keep you company."

I was all for it and invited my sister Margaret to go with us. We didn't take time after the show to remove our makeup and costumes. No one would see us. Getting Margaret Catherine out of bed we went up the hill to the car and watched the boat pull out. We were the last ones there, and it was pitch dark. Buster had left in his car and the last lantern lit wagon load of patrons was moving homeward along the dirt road. We were in the boondocks, miles from nowhere.

The car wouldn't start. "Sounds like we're out of gas. It's been registering full, but the gauge has been acting up lately. I'm afraid it's empty," Harry said.

Then he went to the trunk, got the gas can and hose off the tire pump, and told us, "You girls stay in the car with the doors locked. I saw an old road grader up the road aways when I came in this morning. I'm going to siphon enough gas out of it to get us to a gas station."

I couldn't keep from laughing at the thought of Harry out there in the dark stealing gas. We crouched down in our seats listening to the night sounds of the frogs and crickets and owls hooting in the trees. It wasn't long until Harry was back, saying, "I couldn't get any gas."

Then we saw the headlights of a car coming down the road. It stopped, and the driver stuck his head out the window and asked, "Do you folks need any help?"

"Yes, we ran out of gas," Harry replied.

They were gone quite awhile before Harry returned and we were on our way. Our good Samaritan was a preacher holding a revival meeting back in the hills and was on his way home when he saw us. He invited us to come to the tent meeting the next evening.

We had to travel over rutted roads and creek beds before reaching the main road. Then the going was easier until we turned onto the river road leading down the mountainside to the town below. A heavy fog had moved in off the river and visibility was near zero. As we moved into the valley the going became rougher. At one location Harry stopped the car to get our bearings and nearly stepped out into space, we were on the edge of a cliff. There was no turning back, we had to keep going, feeling and inching our way along. Finally, we became airborne and dropped several feet before hitting bottom.

We spent the night there and met the boat when she arrived the next morning. The townspeople were amazed and told us that no one had driven a car over that road in years. It was an old abandoned river road, partially obstructed with landslides and rocks. It had been replaced by a new road that we had missed in the dense fog.

We had a wonderful time that summer combining work and play touring the Ohio, Cumberland, and Tennessee Rivers with my family and actors on the *Majestic* Showboat.

Chapter 16
My Last Summer on the Showboat

The spring of 1941, Harry took a leave of absence from his job so we could tour with the showboat. "It will keep me from having to send for you later on," Dad said with a pleased grin.

Tommy had quit his job at the shipyards as usual to help Dad ready the boats. Ester took leave from her job at Corrick's Drug Store to serve as cook and ticket taker again. Their two redheaded daughters, Bobbie and Joanne, and Ester's sister, Helen, were also making the tour. With Tommy's two daughters, our Margaret Catherine, Jack, Ruth, John, and Roy, there were a lot of children on the showboat again. Dad couldn't have been happier.

Harry and I took the stateroom on the forward end of the *Atta Boy*. A stairway by our door led up past the pilothouse to the roof deck and calliope, which made it convenient for me.

Rehearsals of *"Her Gypsy Lover,"* got underway with Director Jack Griffeth in charge for his sixth season with the boat. Billy Van, back for his fourth year, was cast in the starring role, and I the co-starring part. Harry and Margaret were second leads; Mrs. Griffeth, Beverly Van, Tommy, Toby Veva, back for his ninth season; and Billy Wade, a radio personality, comedian and dancer, all had parts in the play. After seeing the boats and getting acquainted with everybody, Billy Wade told Dad, "I should be paying you for the privilege of touring with the *Majestic* instead of you paying me."

April 1st, we moved down around "the Point" and pulled into the city wharf at Point Pleasant for the opening night's performance.

With everybody running to the landing and nearby Silver Bridge to watch and listen to the music, I played "The West Virginia Hills" in tribute to our home state, and "Beautiful Ohio" in homage to the immortal river and neighboring state of Ohio on the opposite side of the river. I followed up with "Waiting for the Robert E. Lee, Down Yonder, Steamboat Bill, Basin Street Blues," and "The 12th Street Rag."

I didn't wear asbestos gloves to protect my hands when playing the calliope like some did, the keys were so narrow they got in the way. My hands looked and felt like they'd been run over by a steamroller after not playing for five months. My knuckles were swollen, and my fingertips were blistered. Soaking them in warm water helped relieve the pain and swelling until they formed new calluses and toughened up again. With four more concerts coming up before the show, the condition would worsen before getting any better. This happened each time I went back to playing the instrument, but I loved every minute making people happy with my music, especially Dad.

Tommy, Margaret, Harry and I received a warm welcome. The capacity crowd of hometown folks yelled, whistled, and called us by our names as we entered the orchestra pit and opened the show with our ragtime band.

The play, with gaslight setting, went over for a big hand. Then, with Harry barking the candy sale and handing out the coveted prizes to the lucky winners, the eight act vaudeville revue got underway.

Jack Griffeth, in tuxedo, introduced the acts: A song parody, "When Rose Blows Her Nose, Her Hose Shows," and eccentric dance by Toby Veva; "Country Girl and the Etymologist," Jack and Margaret Griffeth; Solo, "Don't Sit Under the Apple Tree with anyone else but me," and tap dance by Margaret Reynolds; "Traveling Salesman" bit by Billy and Beverly Van; Comedy bit, "There's a Sucker Born Every Minute" by Jack Griffeth, Billy Van, Billy Wade, and Harry; Rhythm Band, "Momma Don't 'Low No Music Playing In Here" by Margaret, Harry, Tommy and myself; monologue and tap dance by Billy Wade, the featured artist.

Moving downriver we played to a full house at Gallipolis, Ohio, then headed up the Kanawha River packing them in at every stop.

At Boncar, W. Va., the mountain scenery was so beautiful we wanted to keep right on going and see what was on the other side. So Dad, Margaret, Margaret Catherine and I hopped in the advance car and Harry took us on a sight-seeing trip to Hawk's Nest State Park. There at the overlook called Lover's Leap, we had a breathtaking view of the towering mountains and New River Canyon. A steam locomotive with a string of coal cars looked like toys in the distance below.

On our way back to the boat the left rear tire blew, the brakes went out and we began running wild down the mountainside. Harry was clinging to the wheel, his foot on the emergency brake. Back and forth we went veering from one side to the other, threatening to go over the cliff or crashing into the mountainside. If that wasn't enough, a Greyhound bus came barrelling up from behind with screeching brakes. Seeing the predicament we were in they were afraid to pass. Luckily, we didn't meet another car or truckload of logs coming up the road. We continued in that manner until we reached the bottom of the mountain, and with a giant sigh of relief, rolled to a stop at a filling station. Dad got a big kick out of telling everybody about it at the supper table that evening.

The Parkersburg News – Showboat *Majestic* Coming Thursday – The *Majestic* will be at the Parkersburg wharf next Thursday, May 8, to show for one week. The *Majestic* has been remodeled, air conditioned, and will be steam heated when necessary. An entirely new company will present a three act comedy drama entitled *"Her Gypsy Lover."* In addition there will be seven acts of vaudeville at no extra charge. The management announces that the *Majestic* is well-known all along the Ohio and its tributaries for having a clean, snappy, up-to-date show the whole family can enjoy. The *Majestic* has national fame, having been featured in Collier's, McCalls, Life, and other magazines.

Revue – Good Crowds at Showboat Here – Despite the unfavorable weather, the *Majestic* Showboat has been presenting shows to good crowds at the waterfront here. "Her Gypsy Lover" and seven acts of vaudeville consisting of songs, dancing and comedy is being enjoyed by the audiences. At the request of the audience, the boat will remain in Parkersburg until next Thursday, May 15. There will be a complete change of program, beginning Monday, when the showboat will present *"Why Wives Worry,"* a hilarious comedy, and seven acts of vaudeville.

After the *Majestic* leaves here, she will show all the towns of any size along the Ohio River, and go up the Monongahela river as far as Fairmont, and other tributaries.

Revue – Program Changed on Showboat – Another good show was enjoyed by the audience of Showboat *Majestic* last evening, with the changing of program. They presented a French Farce Comedy, *"Why Wives Worry"* and seven new acts of vaudeville.

The audience was also surprised and pleased at the appearance of a 4-piece orchestra playing several selections before the show started.

Another surprise was given by Captain Reynolds' son, Tommy, when he did a comedy Russian dance which stopped the show.

The audience has been enlarging each night and it looks as if Mr. Reynolds' amusement palace may remain in Parkersburg indefinitely with the announcement of *"Ten Nights In A Barroom"* to be presented at the request of many of the audience. It is one of the oldest and most popular melodramas that still exists from showboat days gone by.

The showboat is the forerunner of the modern vaudeville tours, and moving pictures and belongs to the past. It is the pioneer of entertainment and the people of Parkersburg can take advantage of the opportunity of attending the only showboat now making one-night stands from a large number that used to show a few years ago."

Showboat to Stay Another Week – "Due to the increasing interest and attendance at the *Majestic* Showboat, Captain Reynolds has decided to remain another week in Parkersburg.

Starting tonight, he will present an old-time melodrama, *"Ten Nights In A Barroom,"* a play that is as popular and as necessary on a showboat as "Uncle Tom's Cabin."

If you have enjoyed either of the plays, don't miss this one, it's old-time speeches and situations will surprise and amuse you. There will also be a complete change of vaudeville."

A capacity crowd gathered on board for the first night showing of *"Ten Nights In A Barroom."* Harry, Tommy, Billy Van, and Jack Griffeth (The Drunkard), were on stage when a windstorm came up. Things began happening on stage that weren't in the script.

The wind hit the boat broadside and slammed her hard into the bank. Tommy left the stage, running to help with the lines. Doubling for him, Harry grabbed up a real bottle instead of the paper prop and whammed it over Billy's head, knocking him out cold.

Then Little Mary (Margaret), appeared at the door pleading, "Father, dear father, come home with me now!"

Angered by her presence in the Inn, the drunkard threw his beer glass at her. It was supposed to have been a sleight of hand throw, but the glass slipped out of his hand. It hit the back wall, with the sound of shattering glass. A sharp piece of glass ricocheted across the stage and hit her, cutting her hand. She let out a bloodcurdling scream, as called for in the script, but she was really cut.

Rushing backstage, Garnett quickly administered first aid and bound the wound tightly so she could return to the stage and play her big deathbed scene.

The curtain parted showing Margaret lying on a cot in center stage. The mother and the drunkard were by her side. What a fine trouper Margaret was! Though in pain, and her wound dripping blood, she portrayed the part with perfect timing and realism to the end.

Forgiving her father, and making him swear that he would never go to the saloon again, she died and went to heaven. Her mother said, "She's more suited for heaven than earth!"

Then the surprised Billy Van revived from his hit on the head, the storm subsided, and the drama was brought to a triumphant curtain finish with the reformed drunk saying, "Free, disenthralled, I stand a man once more!"

Inclement weather with forecasts calling for more of the same followed us everywhere. Heavy rains made the river rise. The higher it got the harder it was for us to navigate.

Finally, Dad told Harry and Tommy, "We're going to have to stop somewhere and wait out the rise. Bill the boat in East Liverpool for one week, beginning June 7, and when you finish, leave the car at the landing and come back by bus. I'll need you both to help move the boats in this high water."

At Wellsville, Ohio, we awoke to find the river out of its banks. It had turned a deep chocolate color and was very swift. All the towboats had laid up to wait out the rise, but Dad wanted to make it to East Liverpool, five and one half miles away.

"We'll never know if we can make it or not until we give it a try," Dad told his helpers. "So, let's bring in the lines and gangplank (half underwater), and give it a whirl."

We were cast loose. Then with Tommy goosing the engine and the boats hugging the shore in calmer water, we began nosing our way upriver. An offshore wind sprang up and we were swept back down across the river into the treetops on the opposite side, at Congo, West Virginia. We stayed there, but presented no show that night.

Next morning gave promise of a beautiful day. Dad, who was making the rounds of staterooms to make sure everybody was up, told me, "We'll be moving out soon. The trip could be dangerous. Take Margaret Catherine over on the showboat and stay there until we land."

After a twenty six hour layover at the emergency landing we headed upriver toward East Liverpool again. This time we continued to hold our own in the current until we tried to pass underneath the channel piers of the City Bridge. There, we were quickly swept back sideways by the crosscurrent swirling around the piers and narrowly missed hitting one of them with the corner bow of the showboat.

With all of us on the upper front deck of the showboat watching, and Tommy back in the engine room goosing the engine, Dad tried to nose her up between the piers again. We were swept back with the showboat listing toward the right side. We miraculously missed hitting the pier. It was just too swift and dangerous. So, running the risk of knocking a hole in the hull on a submerged log, Dad let the boats fall back close to the Ohio shore and succeeded in passing under the bridge between the bank and the first pier. We pulled into the city wharf at East Liverpool moments later.

The landing where Harry parked the advance car was still several feet underwater. We thought the car was ruined, but the owner of a nearby marina had hauled it to the police station when the river started rising.

> *East Liverpool News Review* – Showboat *Majestic* arrives bringing villain and heroine – Once upon a time there was a shrill whistle around the bend and folks of the river community flocked to the wharf as the cry went through the town – "Here Comes the Showboat!"
>
> T. J. Reynolds, owner and manager of the *Majestic* says, "Happy days are here again."
>
> There is a circus atmosphere about the showboat. Candy, peanuts and confections are sold before the curtain goes up and between acts.
>
> "It looks like a big season," Reynolds remarked today as he and his wife, Garnett, counted the receipts of a house Friday night when his troupe opened a week's engagement here.
>
> Reynold's wife, two daughters, a son and son-in-law are members of his company, which included a troupe of 11, of whom two are extras. Mrs. Reynolds has charge of the box office and supervises the kitchen and dining room. A daughter, Margaret, aged 18, plays leading roles and tap dances in a vaudeville feature.
>
> Another daughter, Catherine Reynolds King, age 24, is calliope player and pianist in a four member orchestra.

A son, Thomas Reynolds, is engineer and drummer. Reynold's son-in-law, Harry King, is advance man and doubles brass. Reynolds, a lifetime riverman, is pilot of his boat on which a lone deckhand is employed. The troupe members are recruited from April to October on the Ohio and its tributaries."

One morning the excursion steamer, *Senator,* one of the largest side-wheelers on the western rivers, pulled into the landing next to us. Within an hour two thousand 4-H Clubbers went aboard and she pulled back out taking them on a sight-seeing cruise. Then she laid over at the landing until evening to take out a moonlight excursion of adults for dining and dancing.

Both the *Senator's* calliopist, a tall black man who weighed every bit of 300 pounds, and myself, 5-foot-two in heels and 115 pounds, were scheduled to give alternate concerts that evening. Hundreds of people began arriving early to hear them.

Following my regular schedule, I opened with "Here Comes the Showboat." Before I released the last chord the *Senator's* calliopist began playing "Red Sails in the Sunset."

He was challenging me to a calliope duel, no doubt put up by my father and Captain Posey. I looked at Dad standing on the back deck of the showboat. He was grinning with glee and waving me on. Tommy, who was also in seventh heaven, shoveled coal into the boiler to keep up a full head of steam.

"Over the Waves," I rocked the boat for our side.

"Drifting and Dreaming," he played.

"Beer Barrel Polka," I retaliated.

"There'll be Dancing on the Steamboat Tonight," he replied.

On and on we went, playing one song after the other until he stepped back from the keyboard, and I closed with "The 12th Street Rag."

Shortly after that I was invited by Captain Posey to play his calliope, on the *Senator's* third roof deck. He thanked me and complimented me on my playing, and went on to say, "I'd like to come to the show and watch you perform, but I have to take the boat out again."

East Liverpool Evening Review – Calliope Duel – "It was a battle of calliopes Wednesday night when the excursion steamer *Senator* and the towboat *Atta Boy,* for the Show-boat *Majestic,* gave alternating selections from their steam driven brass sections.

It wasn't so much a battle as a "now it's my turn," for the impresario at the keyboard of the *Senator's* calliope fingered through several selections then the *Atta Boy's* player followed with some old-time favorites.

The *Senator,* with a higher head of steam, of course gave out the loudest, but it seemed the *Atta Boy's* calliope had a higher pitch, which made up for the difference.

The players demonstrated that one doesn't swing calliope tunes. There's an obvious lapse of time between the depressed key and when the lever moves over and opens the steam valve that sends hot jets into the various brass whistles.

But the recital was well received by the hundreds of spectators lining the banks, and autoists blew long blasts on the horns demanding encores."

Review – Plays Packed House – The audience last night filled virtually every one of the *Majestic's* 500 seats, right back to the last row in the small balcony. The customers ate popcorn in huge amounts, meanwhile giving the villain what was one of the most virulent receptions he had ever experienced.

The cast worked under difficulties throughout the first act and some of the second. Alongside was the excursion steamer *Senator,* whose shrieking calliope drowned the lines until she was ready to pull away – and then her dance orchestra and whistle made hearing difficult for another ten minutes.

The players didn't mind. If the noise got too loud they just stood there, and waited – or did a few buck and wing steps – until quiet reigned again. Another time the show was interrupted while one of the actors paged a woman in the audience wanted at home on a "matter of life and death."

He stepped back into his role and asked, "Now, where were we?" and the scene was done again just to make sure no one had missed anything.

Showboat players are one group of actors who can't be temperamental – but they must be versatile. The heroine doubles as candy seller in the intermission, plays saxophone in the orchestra before the show opens, and does a tap dance in the vaudeville turn."

Review – Showboat Held Over – "The showboat *Majestic* due to increasing crowds, is scheduled to remain in East Liverpool another week. This week it is playing an old melodrama *"Ten Nights In A Barroom,"* which has been enjoyed by capacity houses.

The popularity of the boat has been proven by the large number of motorists that gather to hear the steam calliope and inspect the boat and later attend the show. All next week, starting with a matinee Sunday at 2 p.m. the cast will present a farce comedy *"Grandpa's Wedding."*

At Rochester, Pa., we were booked one week and ended up staying two. We could have remained there indefinitely due to popular demand. It was our last upbound stop on the Ohio River.

From there we continued to Monongahela City, Pa. Margaret Griffeth began having severe abdominal pains, and a doctor was called to the boat. He admitted her to the City Hospital, where an emergency operation was performed to remove an intestinal blockage.

The theatre was packed. Billy Wade came on stage, and with tears in his eyes, told the audience, "The show must go on! Mrs. Griffeth, a member of our troupe is lying seriously ill in Memorial Hospital. Jack Griffeth, her husband, is with her and will not be able to perform. Because of the absence of two performers the cast will present a revue instead of the regularly scheduled program. And now – on with the show, maestro!"

Dad was with Jack Griffeth at the hospital. Around midnight he returned with the heartbreaking news that Margaret Griffeth had died.

The following morning, July 22, we moved upriver to Fayette City. We returned to the funeral home at Monongahela City for the funeral service. Her body was temporarily interred in the City Cemetery until it could be moved to Point Pleasant, where Jack intended to stay when he retired from show business.

Margaret Griffeth was a lovely old-fashioned lady, and a great character actress. Everybody who knew her, liked her. She and Jack had been married 25 years.

That evening, and every evening thereafter until we changed programs, I doubled Mrs. Griffeth's parts in the show. It was hilarious. Not only did I play the role of Harry's sweetheart, but that of his mother! A gray marcelled wig and long gingham dress, and makeup, helped me pull it off. I also took her place as Jack's assistant in their fake mind reading specialty.

Due to a bad experience they'd had with an earlier day showboat, Sewickley, Pa., was the only town that had an ordinance prohibiting showboats from stopping there.

Dad told Harry and Tommy, "Talk to the mayor and see if he'll let us bring the showboat in."

The mayor refused saying, "I don't know anything about the reputation of your showboat."

Handing him my large scrapbook full of write-ups and picture layouts, Harry told him, "Take a look at this and you'll see the kind of reputation we have!"

The mayor took his time leafing through the pages, then told them, "Go ahead and post your bills. Your boat will be welcome in our town."

A capacity crowd was on hand for the performance, including the honorable Mayor and his family. They and a wonderful time hissing, booing, laughing, and applauding the acts. After the show the mayor shook Dad's hand and told him, "Captain Reynolds, you have a fine show, and a fine cast of actors. We'll be looking forward to another visit from you. You're welcome to stop here any time."

Billy Van and his wife, Beverly, combed the countryside looking for old graveyards and writing down the comical epitaphs they found on the headstones to use in their act. One was "Here lies the father of 28. There would have been more, but now it's too late." Much to our surprise, they jumped the show, leaving us short three actors.

August found us heading up the Muskingum River after a twelve year absence. We played all the towns to the head of navigation at Philo, Ohio. Then, instead of turning around and working our way back downriver, we continued on up the shallow, log infested stretch of river to Zanesville, Ohio.

Getting the big showboat through the mile long lock canal that runs through the city was the most difficult part of the trip. The showboat and towboat were singularly locked through the miniature size locks.

Harry and Popeye walked along the towpaths helping guide the showboat with ropes. Tommy and Toby Veva were on the head tending the lines. Dad steered the boat by the disconnected ends of the *Atta Boy's* cables. I was on the upper deck telling him when to pull to the right or left, to avoid running aground while backing and filling. We slowly worked our way along the canal.

As the cry, "Showboat's coming up the canal!" spread over the town, the waterfront along both sides of the canal and draw bridges became lined with people.

At the business sections we were stopped dead by sharp curves, tall buildings and bridge abutments bordering the narrow passageway. At the draw span of the famous "Y" bridge, city traffic was backed up for blocks waiting and watching us push, pull, and squeeze the showboat through. The showboat had to be handworked around a hairpin curve and cement obstructions at the railroad drawbridge. Had she been any longer or wider we wouldn't have made it.

At the head of the canal we found a treacherous looking dam spanning the river on he left side of the exit, and a stiff downwind was blowing. A line was run up the shore to help hold us. Then, with one final thrust through the tight exit, we emerged back onto the river. Dad swung the front of the showboat around, facing downstream. Using the *Atta Boy* for a windbreak, he backed her into the landing beneath the Fifth Street Bridge. I was at the calliope heralding our arrival. The time August 25th.

Though it was only nine miles from Philo to Zanesville, due to the unusual circumstances, it took us five hours to make it. There were no public landings above the canal, so Mr. Mast and Mr. Hann graciously let us use their private landing, and moored their cabin cruiser along the *Majestic*. They also gave us free use of their city water.

Radio station WHIZ and newspapers from around the state all generously publicized our arrival at Zanesville.

Zanesville Times Recorder – Steamboat 'Round the Bend – "A sight not seen for many years is that of an old-fashioned showboat coming under the Fifth Street Bridge. Captain T. J. Reynolds, at wheel of Showboat *Majestic,* brings her to safe harbor at Zanesville after one of the toughest river trips on his summer schedule. Narrow locks of Muskingum allowed by inches to spare on either side of boat.

Showboat, itself, lying along the west bank of Muskingum at Zanesville, is its own best advertisement, telling quietly of river romance to passsersby on bridge. While wheelhouse is on the *Majestic,* power is supplied by smaller craft, *Atta Boy,* astern.

Captain Reynolds' pretty daughter, Catherine, admits it makes me a little deaf, now and then, plays calliope on upper deck of *Atta Boy,* beeping out yesteryear's tunes. It's a sure traffic stopper."

Times Recorder – "The showboat *Majestic,* a 120 foot double-decker owned by Captain T. J. Reynolds was open for business today at its dock beneath the Fifth Street bridge.

The boat, propelled by the sturdy little tug, *Atta Boy,* arrived in the upper pool of the Muskingum late yesterday.

Presenting its initial performance last night, the boat's dramatic offering, *"The Lure of the City,"* attracted a sizable crowd.

Captain Reynolds is top man on the showboat *Majestic,* and he knows all the angles of the vaudeville profession. He should, he not only has been in vaudeville 30 years, but he built the *Majestic* in 1923.

The big boat is 34 by 120 feet, but it's not Reynolds' first. He used to leave a wake on the Muskingum years ago with the *Illinois* and *America* Showboats.

The boat visits every tributary of the Ohio River. It is painted every spring and scrubbed twice during the season. The boat starts from Point Pleasant, W. Va., in the spring and ties up again in the fall. The Reynolds live there during the winter.

In addition to the auditorium which seats 500 almost every night, the boat has its own power plant and kitchen, from which meals for the 18 on board are prepared.

Reynolds is 53 now and beginning to get a little gray, but he plans to be in business for a long time to come.

He plans to stay in Zanesville until the crowds get tired of his show, but they've been playing to packed houses every night.

Mr. and Mrs. Reynolds live comfortable in their apartment on the second deck of the big boat. Their back porch at present boasts a bed of vari-colored moss.

In their living room where T. J. enjoys looking over his scrapbook or puffing on a pipeful of Velvet, the Reynolds spend their spare time. The walls are lined with tapestries. A picture of President Roosevelt occupies a prominent place.

Reynolds' violin, which he enjoys playing sometimes, hangs from a nail on the wall. A canary sings in its cage in one corner of the room.

Reynolds' two daughters and sons are also living and working on the showboat. T. J., Jr. was born on the *America.* He doubles on every task on the boat. Sometimes he's deck swab, sometimes engineer, sometimes in the vaudeville troup, he's the drummer in the orchestra."

Columbus Star – The Showboat Comes to Town – "A cargo of Americana-on-the-hoof rides at anchor these days at the foot of the Fifth Street Bridge in Zanesville.

It's a real old-fashioned showboat, and the Muskingum County seat is the farthest upriver into central Ohio such a vessel ever has ventured.

Always an annual treat to those who were fortunate enough to live near our inland waterways, and known to everyone throughout the land by virtue of Edna Verbenas great novel, the showboat carries with it an aura of romance that savors of the nation's past.

Zanesville residents have been listening nightly to the calliope numbers originating aboard the showboat *Majestic*, operated by the Captain's daughter, Mrs. Harry King of Point Pleasant, W. Va. She also appears regularly in the cast of the boat's theatrical offering."

Our crowds continued to increase nightly, so we were held over week after week, where the showboat and crew were a sensation. We played to standing room only the first week, and the second week there were as many people left standing on the bank as there were seated in the theatre. They made runs on the box office during the day reserving their seats ahead for the program changes. They even formed a fan club for Harry and me.

The program changes included *"Why Wives Worry, Ten Nights in a Barroom,"* scenic productions of *"Uncle Tom's Cabin"* and *"The Trail of the Lonesome Pine,"* featuring Harry and me in the leading roles. Daisy Boyington was hired to play Mrs. Griffeth's parts during the rest of the season, and a Miss Sayre the guest star role of Little Eva in *"Uncle Tom's Cabin."* She also did a tap dance in the vaudeville revue. Together we all had 84 vaudeville acts to draw from.

The old-timers who swapped river lore and fishing tales with Dad and Tommy; the people who invited us to after the show parties; the teachers of the private school John and Roy attended, Contractor Mast and Mr. Hann, the dentist; Ray Grossman, former publicity man and drummer for the *Water Queen* Showboat; and all our fans, made this visit memorable. When the final curtain rang down on our spectacular stand in Zanesville, we had been there six weeks.

Taking one last look at our surroundings, we weighed anchor and finished out the remainder of the season revisiting towns on one-night stands to point Pleasant, where we closed the show for the winter.

I didn't know it then, but this was destined to be my last tour with Dad and the *Majestic* Showboat.

Cargo of Memories

Chapter 17
World War II

Following the Japanese sneak attack on Pearl Harbor, December 7, 1941, we became embroiled in World War II. It made many changes in our lives.

There was gas rationing and stricter use of the waterways, the nation's number one source of shipment of raw materials and war goods. Big industrial plants switched from peacetime operation to the manufacture of war materials, and towboats the transportation of same.

The Marietta Manufacturing Plant at Point Pleasant, one of the largest inland marine ways in the nation, was given a government contract to build minesweepers for the Navy. They were shipped via the Ohio and Mississippi Rivers, and Gulf of Mexico, to the Atlantic Ocean.

Guards were posted at all the locks to prevent sabotage. Only those having permits were allowed to make passage. Likewise, no one was allowed off the boats while making lockage. Sightseers that used to run to the locks and watch the boats pass through were strictly forbidden to enter the area. The locks, dams, and bridges along the rivers were vulnerable to enemy attack. Now armed guards protected them.

Men of integrity, not eligible for the draft, were needed to help safeguard the areas in which they lived and traveled. What better person suited for the job and the least suspected of being a Government Agent than Dad. He could be a lookout at our landing and while on tour with the showboat.

Volunteering his services, he was sworn in as a card carrying Secret Service Agent by the U. S. Army Corps of Engineers, Huntington District. He was very proud of the honor of serving his country in this manner.

There was an immediate build-up of our military strength. Men were released from their jobs for combat service. Men and women on the home front teamed up in the production of war materials.

Stamp books were issued to each family to buy sugar, coffee, lard, meat, cheese, etc., by the point system. Housewives had to know how to manage. We didn't throw anything away.

With *Bryant's* Showboat going out of business, the *Hollywood* crushed by ice, and Oscar Bloom's new showboat *Cotton Blossom* destroyed by fire, the *Majestic* was the only showboat left on the Ohio River.

"S' Manthy," a three act comedy drama, featuring Margaret in the title role, was the season's opener at Point Pleasant on April 2, 1942.

The cast was Margaret, Tommy, Toby Veva, Jack Griffeth, Don Dixon – a radio and stage comedian, and Kingsley, a beautiful character actress and musician who took my place as pianist and calliope player.

Following a trip up the Kanawha River the boat stopped at the city wharf for another visit April 25th. *"The G Man,"* was presented to a capacity crowd. They had been playing to full houses every night in spite of the early curfew at all the towns.

Then, following a tour of the upper Ohio, they stopped again for a two day engagement beginning July 27. The comedy drama *"On Treasure Island,"* was the feature.

Margaret Catherine and I were at the landing waiting when the showboat came in. Kingsley was at the calliope playing "That Old Black Magic" and "The Bugle Call Rag."

"The calliope sounded beautiful," I told Dad when we went on board.

"Yes, Kingsley is a fine musician when she's sober. But I can't depend on her worth a damn. After she makes a round of all the bars in town, I don't know if she'll be able to do the show this evening or not. Some of the others are getting out of hand too. It's not the same with you gone. Then, giving me a wishful look, he said, "Ask Harry if he'll come back on the boat and help me finish out the season?"

"All right," I said, and hurried up the hill to the Economy Food Market, where Harry was working as a meat cutter. He listened to me and said, "I'm sorry, Honey, but I just can't quit my job every time your dad needs you. Besides, the season's half over."

"Please go, Dad needs me," I pleaded.

"No, not this time," he replied, and stuck to his guns.

Breaking away from the showboat was very difficult, especially when I knew how badly Dad needed me. For the first time I was torn between my loyalty to Harry and my father, the two men I loved. I had to choose between them. I could take Margaret Catherine, go with Dad and leave Harry. After thinking it over on my walk back to the boat where Dad was waiting, I realized my place was with Harry.

"What did Harry say?" Dad hopefully asked.

"No!" I hated to tell him and let him down so bluntly, and could see his disappointment.

But he took it in his stride, saying, "Harry's a fine man. I was a lot like him, myself, when I was young."

That evening Kingsley was drunk. Not having anyone to take her place, the show went on as scheduled. It was embarrassing in front of the hometown folks. The first time she wobbled and fell off the piano bench playing the overture the audience though she was ill. Then they realized she was drunk and had a good time laughing at her. She staggered on stage and offstage forgetting her cues, ad libbing her lines, hamming it up, teasing the actors, refusing to play their music until she "wanted to" in the vaudeville revue.

But, with Don Dixon receiving most of the credit, there was nothing but praise for the actors in the *Point Pleasant Register* the following day.

Nevertheless, Dad cancelled all other engagements. The uncertainty of getting enough gasoline to run the engine, government red tape, security checks before making lockages with all the other towboats waiting in line, and making him arrive late at the towns. Curfew laws, problems with the cast, and not having his grown children with him to lean on was disheartening. So, he gave up the operation and returned the boats to his landing for the time being.

Tommy, Jr., an expectant father, enlisted in the Navy Seabee division, and served two years in the Pacific. He went ashore in landing barges with his battalion at Okinawa. He entertained his shipmates with comedy monologues, song parodies and Russian dancing. When he returned home, his son, Thomas Jefferson Reynolds, III, was walking. Rounding out his family, Patricia, another redhead, was born a year later.

Wanting something to do, Garnett bought the Economy Food Market on Main Street in downtown Point Pleasant. She operated it for two years. She managed the business affairs and was head clerk. Margaret, and Josephine Bryant, who also wanted something to occupy her spare time in addition to her dance studio, were clerks, etc. Harry was the meat manager. Dad also helped out in his spare time.

Margaret Catherine and I went to the showboat every Saturday morning and looked after Ruth, Jack, John, and Roy until the store closed at 10 o'clock that night.

The store was like home to the customers, old showboat fans, who came in to visit and buy groceries. There was always time for reminiscing and having a laugh or two. Garnett let the mothers leave their infants in banana crates in the back room and watched over them while they shopped.

Garnet was grandma to my Margaret, Tommy and Hazel's four children, Charles, George, Alvina and Billy. She wouldn't have it any other way, though she was too young, being 25 years Dad's junior, and the customers picked it up.

"Hi! Grandma," they'd call to her and ask, "Do you have this, or that today?" Then she'd get it for them.

Dad plowed up his boat landing lot from the top of the riverbank to the street and set out a large victory garden. What they didn't use or give to neighbors he sold in the store to help alleviate some of the shortages.

A reporter asked Dad, "Captain Reynolds, how does the grocery store compare with the showboat business?"

He grinned and told them. "On the showboat we count dollar bills, in the store we count pennies."

Harry and I bought the extra corner lot next to us and the building supplies. Then, with Wes Sealey his helper, Dad built a fine addition to the back of our house.

The West Virginia Ordinance Works for the manufacture of TNT was built just north of us. There was a renewed activity and population growth in the town.

My sister, Margaret, who married Carl Andrew Knopp, was among the first women to don blue jeans and work making electrical equipment at the Sylvania Plant. The women working at Gerlock's Shirt Factory made uniforms and parachutes for the Army. Harry went to work at the Marietta Plant building minesweepers for the Navy, and later transferred to the Chemical Division of the West Virginia Ordinance Works.

Margaret Catherine, who I had taught to read, write and do arithmetic before entering school, was in the first class at the new Ordinance Grade School. It was built in conjunction with the TNT plant to accommodate the new children in the area.

The families who resettled from the TNT area to Bellemeade built the Evangelical United Brethern Church near us. I played piano for their first service and continued to serve as choir director, Primary Superintendent, Director of Youth Work, and head of the Vacation Bible School. Though some members thought I was out of place with my showboat background, I sincerely gave of my time and talents for the good of the community.

I designed and made all of Margaret Catherine's school clothes, and word spread that I could make anything with or without a pattern. Soon I was taking in sewing. I worked in the home instead of the workplace. I specialized in clothing for the oversized and disproportionate figures, the poor, social elites, and the wives of governmental officials. I also made majorette outfits for the Point Pleasant High School marching band.

After selling the grocery store Dad and Garnett moved off the showboat into a new house on Park Street, Counrty Club Addition. Their new home had all the modern conveniences the showboat didn't.

In 1947, at the age of 72, Uncle Tegie had a cerebral hemorrhage and died. Two carloads of us went to the hospital and funeral, where Hazel and I provided the music. Aunt Ida was alone now, not having any children. She bought a house close to Dad. Then he took the *Atta Boy* to Newport, Ky., and brought Ida and her belongings back to Point Pleasant.

One morning Dad sadly told me that old Pal had died. He buried him at the foot of the gangplank. He was sixteen years old and had faithfully served as caretaker of the boats until his death. It was like losing one of the family. Soon, Dad bought another puppy and called him Rebel.

He always came to my house when he needed a haircut. I started cutting his hair when he couldn't find a barber on the Tennessee River tour. He loved to reminisce about our life on the river while I cut and trimmed his almost white hair. He was optimistic about taking the boat on tour with Harry, Tommy, and me again.

Meanwhile he kept the boats in traveling condition. Several times during the summer he leased the *Majestic* to groups who put on shows at the city wharf.

The performances included a matinee and evening showing of the *"Dancing Dolls,"* from New York. I accompanied them at the piano.

The "Fifty-People Minstrel Show" by the Big Bend Minstrel Association had nearly 100 performers, but only 50 could fit on the *Majestic's* stage.

A special presentation of the *"Hatfields and McCoys,"* was directed by Leon Putz, local teacher. Maryln Putz, his daughter, was the leading lady. The show was sponsored by Centra PTA and presented for B&O officials who were in Point Pleasant for the dedication of their new railroad bridge across the Kanawha River. After playing Point Pleasant the showboat was booked in Huntington, W. Va., for a week due to popular request.

Point Pleasant Register – Mrs. King is Calliope Player –
"In fairness to all concerned the Register is of the opinion that a correction should be made publicly concerning who

played the calliope on the showboat *Majestic* during the B&O celebration here May 10.

Mrs. Harry King of Bellemeade, generously contributed her talent at the keyboard of the calliope and provided the proper atmosphere for the presentation of the play, *"The Hatfields and McCoys."* George Strothers, blind pianist and former calliope player on the river, who now resides in Cole Grove, Ohio, didn't come for the celebration, although he was invited. Mrs. King is the daughter of Captain Tom Reynolds, owner of the showboat, and her earlier life was spent on the showboat where she became adept at performing on the calliope and took leading parts in the stage presentations during that time."

The *Majestic* and calliope, with yours truly at the keyboard, were also a part of the Fourth of July, River Days, River Festival, Old Fashioned Bargain Days, Ministerial Celebration, etc. at Point Pleasant.

Bryant's Showboat which had been lying idle at Henderson since 1942, was sold for use as a city wharf-boat at Huntington, West Virginia. It's pilothouse and theatre seats were removed in 1947. It sank during high water the same year.

Now there were only two showboats left, the *Majestic* and the *Goldenrod* moored at St. Louis.

Chapter 18
Under Charter to Kent State University

Dad was on the boat working when he received an unexpected visit from G. Harry Wright, Professor of speech at Kent State University, and his wife, Lila.

He showed them around and told them he was thinking about hiring a professional troupe and taking the *Majestic* on tour again.

Seeing the excellent condition the boats were in, Wright, a showboat enthusiast, had the bright idea of taking her on tour with drama students, operating a school of the theatre.

Though the university couldn't legally supply funds for the operation, they agreed to support the project on a self-sustaining basis. So Dad leased the boat to them along with his advisory and piloting services for a three-month tour.

Fourteen student actors from Kent State and nine from nearby Hiram College were hand picked at auditions to make the trip. The Hiram students were enrolled as Kent State drama students for the summer course, offering six hours of academic credit.

The faculty members were Professor Wright, Director and Manager; Mrs. Wright, Dean of Women and Assistant Manager; Professor Robert I. Pearce, Head of the Hiram College Speech Department, Assistant Director; and Mrs. Pearce, Dietician.

Point Pleasant Register – Showboat Revives Historic Era
– Waitin' at the Levee!
"River folks saw a sight Saturday night that brought back an almost forgotten era in American

history: a showboat under preparation for a summer cruise.

It was the veteran oil-burner *"Majestic,"* being spruced up like an actor who thought he'd never wear grease paint again, and the performers were students from Kent State University.

Under the tutelage of Prof. Manager Harry Wright, they open a three-month series of performances along the river Monday night with that old-time melodrama "Ten Nights in a Barroom."

That show will be staged in Point Pleasant, one of the famed showboat stops of yesteryear. Then the *Majestic,* skippered by Captain T. J. Reynolds will paddle north to hit some of the other towns.

The students will live aboard the vessel throughout the trip and will play sailor as well as actor – scrubbing decks, helping with meals and doing general clean-up work.

A typical 16-hour day will run like this: Work and classes from 7 o'clock breakfast until lunch; rehearsals until 4; then dinner and makeup preparations for the evening show: lights out at 11."

Monday morning, June 7, with Fleice Faust at the calliope keyboard playing "Here Comes the Showboat" and "Cruising Down the River," they pulled into the city wharf.

Then the student band ballyhooed the show uptown, and the Barbershop Quartette were interviewed over the radio, telling about their work on the boat, and entertaining the listeners, including me, with their singing.

Adding to the excitement, the excursion steamer *Avalon* was lying at the landing nose to nose with the *Majestic* drumming up trade. With calliope playing they took out an afternoon excursion, and at 7:15, when the lights came on and the theatre doors opened aboard the *Majestic,* they were back at the landing gearing up to take out a moonlight cruise along the Ohio.

Mrs. Wright was selling tickets. Adults ... $1. Children ... 50¢, tax included. Students in stage costumes and makeup took tickets, ushered, and sold popcorn and soft drinks. By 8:15 all 500 seats in the theatre were filled to the last rows with happy patrons.

Once again, for old-time sake, I was the guest calliopist and Tommy and I were invited to play the overture for the show.

Then the Kent State curtain went up on the play, *"Ten Nights in a Barroom."* The students' portrayal of the "Drunkard," his wife, and terminally ill daughter, Mary, and supporting cast was highly pleasing to the audience.

The two guest stars from Dayton, Stan Mouse and Bill Gusiewite did "Casey at the Bat" and take-off on television, and huckstered candy.

The vaudeville: Professor Wright in skunk tail cap on backwards, and Stan and Bill hammed it up for hilarious laughter. The "Four Mugs and a Brush" sang quartet numbers. Fleice Faust scored with her novelty dance. The Men's Tumbling Team performed. Stan returned to sing "Does Your Mother Know You're Out, Cecelia?" And the finale closing with everybody singing "Ol' Man River" and "Here Comes the Showboat."

Going to the front of the boat, where he said that he "felt very much like a minister standing at his church door saying good-by to his congregation after a particularly successful sermon," Professor Wright shook hands and received congratulations from the crowd as they left the theatre. He also thanked me and invited me to join them for the tour.

Prof. Robert I. Pearce, Mrs. Pearce, their teenage daughter, and the nine Hiram College students who had to wait until their school let out, joined the boat at Charleston, W. Va., bringing the number of people now on board to 33, plus three dogs.

Following a two week stay at Charleston, they worked their way back to Point Pleasant for their return engagement under the auspices of the Point Pleasant Fire Department, Tuesday, July 6th.

Margaret Catherine and I were on hand to see the boat come in. What a beautiful sight! She moved out of the mouth of the Kanawha with Dad at the helm. Faculty and students lined the decks. Two male students were helping Tommy and John with the lines as they pulled into the landing with calliope playing.

The showboat parade was staged uptown led by the drum majorette. Then the marching band walked two miles inland from the river and surprised Dad and Garnett with a serenade outside their home, bringing all the neighbors out to watch. Garnett invited them all inside for cake and coffee.

That evening, in addition to the calliope concerts, including one by me, the Dixieland Jazz Band performed on the forward roof deck of the showboat prior to the show.

By 8:15 there wasn't a vacant seat or standing room left in the theatre. Piano and drum music opened the show. It was the setting of the New York smash hit, *You Can't Take It With You.* The cast received a standing ovation as the final curtain closed on "Grandpa," Prof. Pearce, saying grace at the table.

The prize candy sale and Sing-Along was next, followed by four vaudeville specialties and Prof. Pearce in beautiful baritone voice singing "Ol' Man River," and all the rest of the cast joining the chorus and the finale, "Here Comes the Showboat!" for another standing ovation.

Continuing upbound on the Ohio River they played to sold out houses and turned hundreds of people away nightly at Parkersburg and Wheeling, West Virginia, and East Liverpool, Ohio. Then they worked their way back downriver, bypassing Point Pleasant, and stopped at Gallipolis, Ohio. Harry, Margaret Catherine and I visited the boat. They were presenting the play *"Our Town."*

It was mid-August, and the students had learned to act under the tutelage of Professor Wright and Pearce, made stage, radio and television appearances, posted bills, and absorbed river lore from Dad, all working on "the world's last traveling showboat."

Tommy and John showed them all the fun and tricks of diving and swimming off the boats and paddle wheel. We could hear them laughing and splashing in the river when we drove up to the city wharf. Dad was sitting on the checkpost keeping a fatherly watch over them, just as he used to do with his own children.

From Gallipolis they worked their way downriver to Cincinnati, where they tied up at the foot of Lawrence Street for a closing ten day engagement.

Tommy told me, "We were held up at the locks, waiting for three steamboats and their barges to make lockage, and didn't get there until five o'clock that evening. A man was waiting to hook up a phone in the ticket office. Soon every seat was sold out for the entire ten days. I needed a baseball bat to keep the people who wanted to buy tickets off the boat. But we could just get so many on, and that was that!"

When the show closed at Cincinnati, September 15, it was back to school for the students and their professors. During their fourteen and one half weeks tour, they gave 92 performances and entertained up to 35,000 patrons.

In addition to earning university credit and getting unique training in show business, the students and their professors had accomplished what they set out to do: "Revive the showboat with a new flair and bring back some of the cultural heritage of America."

Back in harbor, Dad, Tommy, and two laborers removed the 40hp engine from the *Atta Boy* and replaced it with a 135hp Caterpillar diesel motor for safer and more efficient transportation of the showboat. But, when he took the *Atta Boy* for a trial run the engine nearly ran her under. It was too powerful for the boat, so he installed a governor on the engine and it worked as expected.

Chapter 19
Hiram College Showboat
Players 1949-1950

Both Kent State University and Hiram College wanted to lease the *Majestic* for separate tours that spring. Professor and Mrs. Wright wanted it for another three-month tour, but Dad let Hiram College have it for a longer five-month tour and more money. It would begin April 30 and end October 1st.

Hiram College's Summer School Bulletin read:

"230 – Operating Theatre Aboard the Showboat *Majestic* 6 Semester Hours – Students receiving training and performance while living on the only moving showboat left in the country. A unique experience for both major and non-majors with the personnel, playing to some 50 odd towns along the Ohio and tributary rivers, this cruise offers practical training in theatre productions, as well as fostering such personality characteristics as poise, responsibility and cooperativeness. Class limited to 15 students each term.

There will be no theoretical study of drama, except as theory directly affects the practical job being done. There will be no examinations.

The classroom will be the showboat *Majestic* and the broad expanses of the Ohio River Systems. The class period lasts twenty four hours a day, as the students, in the best tradition of the traveling theatre will eat, sleep, and live for the show."

Twenty four students were chosen to participate in the venture. Half would be on board each semester. Also on board were Prof. Robert Pearce, his wife, their son, Jack, and his friend, Dick Underwood (who were still in high school and were helpers around the boat), and Mrs. Pearl Switzer "Aunt Pearl," cook; Dad, Bud Lee Meaige (who married my sister Ruth), and 16-year-old John as Dad's helpers.

April 30, 1949, they opened the show at Point Pleasant. From my front porch that evening we could faintly hear Bill Reynard, the student calliopist, playing "Over the Waves, Little Annie Rooney," and a "Bird in a Gilded Cage." I was scheduled to play one of the calliope concerts that evening, so Harry, Margaret Catherine and I headed for the showboat.

The Dixieland Jazz Band performed on the roof deck of the showboat before the lights came on. The band opened the show. Then the curtain opened on *The Drunkard*," followed by the candy sale and six sparkling acts of vaudeville, and grand finale.

Working their way upbound on the Ohio, where they played double engagements with the excursion *Avalon*, they continued to draw capacity houses at every stop.

Alternating *The Drunkard*" with *You Can't Take It With You*," and *Arsenic and Old Lace*," along with new lines of vaudeville and Children's Matinee performances of *Hansel and Gretel*" or *Cinderella*," they played one- to three-week stands enroute to Pittsburgh. They finished the remainder of the season visiting towns south to Louisville, Ky. The show closed there.

In commemoration of Hire College's one hundredth anniversary, the *Majestic* was leased to them again for another five-month tour the spring of 1950.

Hiram's Centennial book had this to say about Dad. "To the Hiram Players and their professors, Captain Reynolds is an encyclopedia of river and showboat lore. The itinerary for the trip was planned by him, and the entertainment itself is from the old showboat tradition in which he grew up.

To students on the *Majestic*, Captain Reynolds offers in effect, a course of his own in the history and techniques of that sometimes neglected section of the American theatre that has been his life and work."

Professor Pearce headed the showboat project again, Assistant Professor, Douglas Mitchel, was technical director.

He also designed and built the stage scenery, directed the marionette shows, and appeared in revues.

Paul Henderson, a senior student, was the business manager of the showboat project. Mrs. Pearce was house mother and dean of women, Aunt Pearl dietician and cook. Jack Pearce, and Dick Underwood, helpers, John and Bud Meaige Dad's helpers.

"The Drunkard" and *"John Loves Mary"* were alternately presented with vaudeville specialties and marionette shows during the season.

After opening the show at Point Pleasant they toured the Kanawha River and Upper Ohio to Pittsburgh, and the lower Ohio. During a one week stop at Cattlettsburg, Kentucky where Showboating was the theme of their Centennial program, the *Majestic* and Hiram Players aided in the observances. The show closed at Louisville, Ky., October 1st. Over 40,000 people attended and saw their shows that season.

Cargo of Memories

Chapter 20
The River Players

The *Majestic* was under charter to a private group of professors and students from colleges in Ohio and North Carolina in the spring of 1951. Some of the students were veterans from touring with the boat the previous three seasons. Called "The River Players," Wes Egan, assistant professor of speech at Kent State University, was the director of the shows.

The three-act comedy drama *"Lure of the City,"* and six vaudeville specialties were the season's opener at Point Pleasant, May 21, 1951. From there they made one- to three-day stands upbound on the Ohio to Pittsburgh, Pa., then headed south with a change of program to Paducah, Kentucky, where they played a 3-day engagement at the foot of Broadway on August 30-31 and September 1st.

From there they made an adventurous trip up the Cumberland River to Nashville, Tennessee, where the show closed October 1st.

They operated nineteen weeks and gave 133 performances to over 50,000 people.

Cargo of Memories

Chapter 21
Hiram College Players
1952 – 1959

The following spring the *Majestic* headed out on a five-month tour with Hiram College again. Twenty-four student actors were on board.

Their repertoire included *"The Drunkard, Murder in the Red Barn, Under the Gaslight, The Vengence of Emory Blacksloth,"* and *"Ten Nights in a Barroom."*

After opening the show at Point Pleasant June 7, they worked their way up the Ohio River to Rochester, Pa. The were held over for a month due to popular request. Then they worked their way up the Monongahela River to Fairmont, W. Va. The showboat hadn't been seen or the calliope heard since I played it there in 1941.

They played Pittsburgh for four weeks and closed the season there October 6th. While there, a woman leaped off the Sixth Street Bridge and was rescued by a male student. Dad and Tommy picked them up in the skiff and brought them back to the showboat where the emergency squad was waiting.

The *Majestic* was under seasonal charter to Hiram College for the next six years. They secured the lease at the close of each season to keep other groups from getting the boats. With Dad at the helm and Doug Michell heading the project, the *Majestic* just kept rolling along like "Ol' Man River."

> Mademoiselle Magazine – 1953 – Rounding the bend, approaching like a queen, floats a two-decker white painted showboat. Riverboat characters in gay nineties

costumes leaned against the railing, cheering and shout-
ing above the noise of the calliope. Then the gangplank
swung out and a little band of clarinetists, trumpeters
and circus parade drummers come ashore with troupes
following in noisy hullabaloo. The spectators, young and
old, cheer. Once again the river assumed it's role as usher
of an American brand of excitement called "Showboat."

Old-time melodrama and vaudeville are still brought
to towns along the Ohio River by the showboat *Majestic*,
sole survivor of a once great tradition. Owned and navigated by Captain T. J. Reynolds, a vigorous man with
twinkling eyes. As the last of her kind, the *Majestic* still
packs the house. Reynolds makes many of the living rules
for the Hiram College students and keeps an eye on the
accounts. For a man who has survived all his competitors,
the depression, and high costs, this means a chance to
continue "the only life he loves."

Dad was in his element being the fatherly overseer of the college
students from season to season. "They reminded me of you kids and
I've had a good time with them," he told me.

The students loved to gather at his feet and listen to him
reminisce about his life and times on the river. In his quiet way he
kept the *Majestic* going and won the admiration and friendship of the
crew.

Dressed in his casual clothes and straw hat he even let the
students talk him into marching in the showboat parade with them.
He was often the other half of the *Showboat* banner bearers.

The temperature was around 100 degrees during their visit at
Wellsville, Ohio, and instead of marching he and Aunt Pearl rode in
a stagecoach provided by the city. While there, he also gave *Majestic*
memorabilia to the Wellsville River Museum.

Wellsville Press – June 28, 1956 – "Showboat Moves On
– Monday morning about 6:40 the *Majestic* pulled out to
move upriver. I (the reporter, Raymond Crumbley) was
aboard thanks to the kindness of Captain T. J. Reynolds,
to find for myself the feeling of riding the river.

Haze drifted up from the hollows across the river, and
a brisk breeze sailed the last of the dark clouds over the
hills. The chill air forced the last traces of sleep from my
eyes as we backed into the current.

The water was muddy and swift from the heavy rain,
but Captain Reynolds nosed her out and relaxed to ride

the familiar route upstream. I wondered about the current, but he leaned back and chatted with me, steering easily with his foot on the wheel.

As we rode upstream, the actors and actresses of the night before began to stir and get ready for breakfast. I had coffee with the Captain and some of the cast while we churned toward the Newell bridge.

It was around 8 a.m. when we docked at East Liverpool, and there was a hustle to secure lines. The deck was swept and scrubbed and the auditorium was cleaned for another performance. The call came for "Uncle Tom" to get on stage; and the other half of the show business, really the only half, began again.

As I walked up Broadway from the landing, a few curious people began to gather by the calliope's "Margie" and "Has Anybody Seen My Gal?" I hated to break the spell and wondered how I could ride the bus again after the glamor of the *Majestic* and its hard-working crew."

In October, 1956, and yours truly, calliopist, the *Majestic* hosted a full-scale musical show in connection with the celebration of the 182nd anniversary of the Battle of Point Pleasant.

Meanwhile, Harry and I watched Margaret Catherine grow into a lovely young woman and marry Ellis Paul Hudson, a Gallipolis, Ohio native. They made their home in Prospect, Ohio.

The morning after the wedding, Dad caught me crying. One look at Margaret's empty room and he knew why. Leaning against the kitchen countertop he tenderly told me, "Catherine, children grow up and you have to let them go when they are ready. It's like a mother bird with her babies. She devotes all her time to feeding and caring for them, even pushing them out of the nest when they're old enough to fly. Soon they can fend for themselves and have families of their own. It is nature, and the plan of things." He made me feel better, as he had all my life.

Point Pleasant Register – "The *Majestic* coming back again as a 15 week tour starts June 11, 1958 – Residents of this area and along the Ohio River will hear an old familiar note of music next week when the only show now traveling on the rivers will start a 15 week journey stopping for one night stands.

The *Majestic* showboat will dock June 11 at the Fourth street landing for the opening of the season. *"The Poor of New York"* will be presented by Hiram College Players.

Captain T. J. Reynolds of Point Pleasant, owner of the *Majestic* said that he and his son, Tommy, are painting and cleaning the boats and plan to have the work completed when the troupe arrives Saturday.

Captain Reynolds and his son will operate the diesel boat during the tour."

From Point Pleasant they made a round-trip tour of towns along the Kanawha River, then worked their way upbound on the Ohio to Pittsburgh.

Pittsburgh Press – Showboat *Majestic* Makes River Rock – August 5, 1958 – "Using the good ship *Majestic* for the theatre, a crew of Hiram College, Ohio, students have brought showboat into Pittsburgh for an indefinite stay.

If the first week's menu of theatrical "ham" is an accurate guidestick of what's in the student's bag of tricks, the old Allegheny River will be rocking every night.

For in *"Poor of New York,"* the performers stop at nothing to provide evening's entertainment. Off stage remarks are plentiful, as are audience baiting, heckling and an assortment of fun filled antics.

Responding to the audience, the players, who literally are jacks of all trades aboard the vessel, give their all to make the two hours pleasure filled. Comfort, too, is keynoted early as the audience is told to take off coats, unbutton shoes, loosen ties and relax.

Melodrama is only one part of the good times aboard the showboat. A vaudeville show featuring seven or eight acts is featured nightly as is the "old time, all time, good time, whizbang candy sale."

This sale is beyond description. But if it's entertainment you 're seeking, you can't go wrong.

The two favorite vaudeville numbers are Barbershop quartette and Dixieland band. The latter's finale of "Saints Go Marching In" is a rouser that makes the *Majestic* bounce from stem to stern.

"Poor of New York" will continue Saturday and next week's production will be *"Murder in the Red Barn."* Other melodramas to follow include *"Ten Nights in a Barroom"* and *"Hawkshaw the Detective."*

A different set of vaudeville acts is featured on each program, so there is a complete new show each week. And

when its the *Majestic* crew of Hiram caperers performing, something is always happening on the river."

My brother, John, sang with the Men's Chorus, and played
boogie-woogie calliope duets with the male student calliopist during
the season. He played bass. He also met and married Juanita
Randolph, a hometown girl, and continued to tour with the boat while
she stayed at home and visited him.

My brother, Roy, who attended Hiram College on a scholarship,
also met and married Barbara, a student thespian, in 1958.

The show closed September 11. When the curtain rang down it
also marked the end of Hiram's operation with the *Majestic* showboat.

During their long, record breaking run with the *Majestic*, Hiram
College estimated that nearly 400,000 people saw their performances
aboard the showboat.

A motion picture was made of the Hiram Showboat operation
during the tour and was shown overseas as part of an educational and
cultural exchange.

After the Hiram group left, Dad leased the showboat to the
Kroger Company for the filming of a television commercial at Pittsburgh. During this time the name *Majestic* was covered and she wore
a banner that said *Kroger Top Value Showboat*.

Kroger officials and dignitaries gathered on board. Then with
the cameras rolling, Dad slowly nosed the showboat down out of the
mouth of the Allegheny, around "the Point" on the Ohio, and up the
mouth of the Monongahela River, advertising their new brand of
"Showboat – Live Better for Less" products.

Cargo of Memories

Chapter 22
End of an Era
1959

That spring, the *Majestic* was taken out on the ways at the Marietta Plant for repairs to her hull, which was leaking from dry rot again. Her lower gunnels and bottom planks were replaced. The tab was $16,000. Dad returned her to the landing sound as a dollar.

The following morning he came to our house and told me, "Catherine, I just finished taking the showboat back to the Marietta Plant."

"What for?" I asked with surprise.

"The river was falling and I had to shove the boats a good piece away from the bank before going home last evening. The back part of the boats went out easy, but the front wouldn't budge. So, I kept pushing and prying on it until it did move – and it looked like the showboat dropped down. I had never seen the boat do that before. Thinking it was only my imagination, I anchored her there and went up the hill to the car.

"I was driving away when I just happened to glance back down at the boats. The showboat looked like she was setting low in the water. So, I stopped the car and went back and looked down the front hatch. A tree stump was sticking up through the bottom of the hull, near the centerfront of the boat, and floodwater was gushing in around the hole. The boat had settled down on the stump. When I kept prying and shoving on her the stump came up through the new bottom planks.

"It was getting dark and there was no one in sight on the bank that I could call for help. So, I went down inside of the hull with the lantern, lumber, saw, hammer and some nails and built a bulkhead around the hole and stump. It kept the water from coming in until the locks raised the river to float her off the stump. It was a good thing I went back to check on the boat, or I would have found her sunk this morning. Mr. Windsor (President of the company) took the boat out on the ways and is repairing the damage free," he said.

Day after day he returned to the boat to work. Rebel, his German shepherd was always with him. Using block and tackle to shift the heavy loads, he put new support timbers and floor boards on the main deck of the showboat. He also replaced the single door emergency exits with double doors on each side of the auditorium, and built escape hatchways on both sides of the upper deck for crew members.

Instead of accepting an offer from another college or group wanting to lease the showboat for the summer, Dad put the *Majestic* and *Atta Boy* up for sale. He was 71 years old, with his eyesight and hearing failing. After 62 years of working on the river, and 47 years of bringing theatre to river towns with the *Illinois, America* and *Majestic Showboats*, he was quitting the business.

His first advertisement, with a beautiful picture of the Majestic in transit on the river, appeared in the *Waterways Journal*. Then all the news media, including the *New York Times*, radio, and television carried the story. He also made several television appearances and made a tape for *Voice of America*, telling about his life on the river.

When a reporter implied that he was quitting the operation because showboat business isn't what it used to be, he curtly replied, "It's better today than any time before the depression. The audiences are there waiting for someone to bring the showboat around again.

"The *Majestic* has returned a profit every year since I built her in the fall and winter of 1922-23. That year there were fourteen showboats on the rivers.

"Folks in the river towns have always enjoyed old fashioned melodramas. Even in Cincinnati they enjoyed *"East Lynn,"* the Toby plays, and *"Saintly Hypocrites and Honest Sinners."*

"Showboats aren't one of those hollowed out stern wheel steamers Edna Ferber talked about, a real showboat is a barge and has to be towed by a tugboat. Most of all, it's a matter of keeping a historic institution alive and prosperous for the enjoyment of plain people."

A number of offers came in from individuals and organizations wanting to buy one or both the boats, or just the calliope. He could have made a quick sale, but waited for the right person who wanted to buy the complete outfit and operate them in the old traditional manner, as he'd always done.

That special person was Dr. Lee Norville, President of Indiana University, at Bloomington, Indiana. Dad showed him the boats from stem to stern and explained their operation. He wanted to buy them as an addition to the Brown County Playhouse they operated as a summer theatre.

Dad told him he wanted $30,000 for the boats and that they would make their money back in less than three seasons.

"Will you take ten thousand dollars down and the rest in two yearly installments? But before I can make a commitment, I'll have to get permission of the university," he said.

"I don't know anything about you fellows, I wonder if I can trust you?" Dad replied.

"You know as much about us as we know about you. Can I trust you?"

Dad smiled, shook his hand, and said, "I'll trust you, Dr. Norville."

August 11, 1959, the *Majestic* and *Atta Boy* became the property of Indiana University with J. A. Franklin, vice president, closing the deal. Dad also signed a contract to accompany the faculty and students on their first summer tour with the showboat as Captain and advisor, to assure a smooth take over. He also agreed to oversee the steel hull being installed on the *Atta Boy*, at the Marietta Plant. It cost $44,000, bringing their total investment in the two boats to $70,000.

Shortly after this Dad told me, "A man from Warner Brothers came to the house yesterday and asked if I'd sign a contract for them to make a movie of my life on the river, and it includes you. They want you to play the calliope and piano, and the adult role of yourself in the movie. I'm thinking about it, we might be in a color moving picture show."

But he didn't get to sign the contract. December 16, 1959, I answered the phone and heard, "Catherine, I have bad news for you ... your father is dead. He fell off the boat into the river and drowned."

He had gone to the showboat in the early afternoon and didn't come home the usual time that evening. So, Garnett called Tommy, who lived across the river from the boat landing, and asked him to go check on Dad. His car and Rebel were there, but Dad was nowhere in sight. Finding a guardrail broken on the side deck of the *Atta Boy*, Tommy called the Volunteer Fire Department Emergency Squad, of which he was a member, to the scene.

It was thought that Dad was attempting to start an engine which had an outside crank, had a heart attack and fell into the Kanawha River. Paul Woods, Fire Chief, found his body in 25 feet of water, thirty feet between the *Atta Boy* and the shoreline. Tommy helped pull his body out of the river. His death was ruled accidental drowning.

It was ironic that his life would end that way, the only person to drown off any of his boats. The river was his life, and his destiny.

I was crushed with grief. I didn't cry. I couldn't. Only death could sever the wonderful father and daughter relationship we shared.

Newspapers, radio and television carried the story of Captain Tom Reynolds, of showboat fame, accidentally drowned.

Flowers, telegrams, and expressions of sympathy poured in from friends, actors who had toured with the boat, college, and acquaintances from all over the world. The funeral was held at the Presbyterian Church in Point Pleasant. Reverends David Parr and Jack Higgens, officiated.

Burial was in Suncrest Cemetery. His death marked an end to an era in Showboat Americana. A tombstone marks his grave.

Dad was the last of the old time showboat operators. He was a pioneer craftsman and showman. A dynamo of energy, he used brawn and intellect instead of book learning to achieve a goal. In his easygoing, independent way he reached the pinnacle of showboating success. He was unique since he built, piloted, captained, and maintained his own boats.

The *Majestic* was the longest running showboat on the river under the same owner. Dad was also the only showboat operator to tour with a university and college troupe. He held the record for raising the largest family, five boys and four girls aboard the showboats *Illinois, America* and *Majestic*. He carried the largest professional crew each season, eight or more, in addition to the family actors and musicians. He also put on some of the best shows. The *Majestic* showboat never folded up because of lack of business, even during the worst years of the depression. When he had to pay his actors out of his pocket to stay afloat, he kept going and ended every season in the black.

Regrettably, this left Indiana University without Dad's help for their upcoming season. Though no one could ever take his place, my brothers, Captain Carl Jackson Reynolds, Master pilot for the Ohio and Mississippi River Valley Line, Capt. John Reynolds, pilot for the same company, and Roy Reynolds, their helper, agreed to honor Dad's contract as trip pilots for the university during time off from their regular jobs that summer.

Chapter 23
Famous Showboat Leaves Home Waters

Point Pleasant Register – Thursday, May 5, 1960 – "It was a sad day for Mason County riverboat fans as the famous *Majestic* prepared to leave its home port for new waters. Like a favorite son getting a glorious but somewhat sad send-off from the family, as he seeks greater fame, the *Majestic* received a warm farewell from Mason Countians.

The departure was delayed 17 hours until Captain Carl J. Reynolds arrived from Memphis to take the wheel. The banks of the Kanawha were lined with well wishers who arrived early to say goodbye to the hulky lady of the theatre which has graced its shores for over a quarter century. But, no one seemed to mind when moving time was delayed. It was like a reprieve.

Children were dismissed from the school in Henderson to see the passage of the last showboat on the Ohio.

A celebration, under the direction of Mayor Archie Henry of Henderson and the town folks, staged a farewell program.

The program started with the Point Pleasant High School Band, directed by Norman Coffman, leading the parade from the Shadle Bridge through town to the boat landing where a speaker's stand was set up. Floats carrying themes "Good-bye Showboat *Majestic*" were in the Parade. A float depicted the days when area folk attended the showboat performances years ago along the Ohio and Kanawha Rivers. The float was pulled by a team of mules driven by Clarence Meaige (Bud's brother) and his wife, who were attired in an outfit popular at the turn of the century. Also participating in the parade were the students and teachers of Henderson School.

Mrs. T. J. Reynolds, widow of the *Majestic's* former owner, speaking at the ceremony said, "It's hard to say anything, I am too sad."

Archie Henry spoke briefly and introduced Senator Hubert Humphery, on his presidential campaign stop in Henderson. He had spoken prior to the celebration. "I once attended showboats on the Mississippi River," he told Garnett. Paul Crabtree, Secretary of Congress, and Rep. Ken Heckler was introduced. Herbert Miller, Director of Point Pleasant Chamber of Commerce, spoke briefly.

The High School band played "Hail, Hail, the Gang's All Here, Sailing, Sailing," and "Floating Down the River."

C. N. Haddox, Mason County Schools Music Director and television personality, played the calliope as the fans listened for the last time to it's echoes.

The Showboat *Majestic* then moved from it's Henderson landing and headed for Madison, Indiana. At the Majestic's stern the sturdy little towboat *Atta Boy* churned the Kanawha and Ohio Rivers into a white wake, like someone hurrying away from a loved one before they broke into tears."

Point Pleasant Register – Last Showboat on Ohio Preserves an Era – Madison, Ind. – "Guaranteeing that the colorful showboat will not completely disappear from the national scene for another "straw hat circuit" of summer theatre, Indiana University and a troupe of campus actors this summer have assured that the last of the Ohio River touring showboats, as the venerable *Majestic*, still will be in operation."

Twenty-six versatile actors were chosen to make the tour, thirteen during the first half of the season and thirteen the second half. The faculty and crew included Dr. Lee Norville, Executive Director; William E. Winzer, as director; Gene Parola, alternate director; four university staff members, and a chief cook.

They trimmed the boats in red paint, installed Indiana University signboards on the showboat and changed the *Atta Boy's* name to

"*IU*" for the university. They also beautified the stage with a painted grand drop curtain depicting the Indiana University Showboat *Majestic* in transit on the river.

They opened the show at Madison, Indiana, June 8. the band performed, then, holding true to tradition, they presented "*Ten Nights in a Barroom,*" followed by the prize candy sale, variety show, and grand finale.

Their alternate dramas were "*In Old Kentucky*" and "*The Taming of the Shrew.*" The Indiana Players gave eighty-eight performances in twenty-seven Indiana and Kentucky towns. They included four day stops in Owensboro and Henderson, three weeks at Evansville, and a three-week closing stand at Louisville, September third. Then the boats were moved across the river to their new berth on the Jeffersonville water front.

The comedy drama, "*Peg O' My Heart,*" was their season's opener June 1, 1961, at Jeffersonville. They worked their way upbound on the Ohio to Cincinnati for a nine day stand.

I didn't know the showboat was in Cincinnati until I turned on the radio. The announcer asked, "After you leave here will you take the showboat on the Mississippi River?"

"Yes, we'll be showing Wickliffe, Columbus, and Hickman, Ky., and Belmont, Missouri," one of the students replied.

"How will you get the showboat on the Mississippi river from here?" the announcer wanted to know.

He made it sound so easy, "We just keep going down the Ohio until we come to the end of the river, then we turn left."

Presenting the alternate drama "*Old Soak,*" the *Majestic* continued on her 1,000 mile tour. It was the showboat's first appearance on the Mighty Mississippi River, the only showboat seen in the area since the *Goldenrod* stopped there with a Major Bowe's Amateur Unit in 1937, before going into permanent stock at St. Louis. Indiana University successfully operated the *Majestic* for seven years. The first five years were traditionally spent making one night to three week stands along the Ohio and Mississippi Rivers. The last two years were spent at Jeffersonville due to the deterioration of the *Majestic's* hull and failure to pass her safety at sea test. They were allowed to continue showing in the safety of the harbor.

Their repertoire of plays included "*East Lynn, Charley's Aunt, The Drunkard, Arsenic and Old Lace, Rip Van Winkle, On Borrowed Time,*" and "*The Barker.*"

During that time more than one hundred Indiana University students were on the showboat gaining acting experience and academic credits. Over 150,000 people saw their performances.

In 1967, Dr. Moody, Director of the Theatre Department, cancelled the operation. To continue they would have to dry dock the *Majestic* for costly repairs. Choosing between their affection for the grand old showboat and practicality. They wanted to build another showboat, but got an estimate of one million dollars. It was too much money. So, they put the *Majestic* and *IU (Atta Boy)* up for sale to the highest bidder.

September 1967, the city of Cincinnati purchased *Majestic* and *IU* for $13,500 for use as a major attraction in their new Riverfront Park.

The calliope, pilot wheel from the *Majestic*, her nameboard, and anchor weren't included in the sale.

Chapter 24
At the Foot of Broadway

Seepage water was pumped from the *Majestic's* bilges and further checks were made of the boats before setting out on their 132 mile trip to their new home in Cincinnati. The Captain, engineer, a deckhand, and two representatives of the city were on board. All went well for five miles. Then the *Atta Boy's* paddle wheel began falling apart, killing the engine, and they were left stranded in the middle of the river.

Drifting with the wind and current they came to a stop on the Kentucky side of the river, where they spent the night. Next morning the Tugboat *"K"* arrived from Cincinnati and transported them the rest of the way to the Queen City.

Upon arrival the showboat and towboat were harbored in the protective waters of the Four Seasons Marina.

October 13, 1967, a "Here Comes the Showboat Revue" was presented aboard the boat as a welcoming ceremony for the new owners and all others who had a part in bringing the showboat to Cincinnati.

Paul Rutledge, of the University of Cincinnati's Arts and Sciences, signed a contract with the city to produce the shows. Students and professionals from Cincinnati were cast members. Graduate students were in charge of the technical and business office. Richard "Rick" Diehl, General Manager.

Their first summer season, while still moored at the marina, included five musicals: *"Anything Goes,"* beginning March 31, 1968, and running through Saturday of each week, for three weeks, with vaudeville featured on Tuesdays and classic films on Saturdays. *"Riverwind, The Boy Friend, Bells Are Ringing"* and *"110 In The Shade"* were the following presentations.

Single ticket prices – Wednesdays, Thursdays and Sundays $3.25. Fridays and Saturdays $3.75. Subscription Prices – Wednesdays, Thursdays or Sundays $13.00. Fridays or Saturdays $15.00.

That fall and winter of 1968-69, the *Majestic* was fitted with a steel hull at the Tucker Marine, Inc. for $44,800. It was a steel casing, under which the old wooden hull Dad installed himself in 1939, is visible below deck. The steel hull extended the length and breadth of the *Majestic* to 135 by 40 feet.

Inside the theatre the orchestra pit and box seats were removed to enlarge the stage from 12 by 20 feet to 20 by 24 feet. The balcony seats were removed for the installation of a lighting booth, central air, heating, and a sprinkling system for fire protection. The old wooden opera seats were removed and replaced with red upholstered seats. They reduced the 500 seating capacity to 233 people, main floor seating only. Red carpet adorned the aisles and balcony windows and ceilings were painted black to darken the theatre for matinee performances. It was given new coats of red and white paint, and with flags waving in the breeze along the top decks of the boats, they looked like new again.

The work was done under a $100,000 program for the restoration and preservation for the *Majestic* as a historic structure. The amount was budgeted for the riverfront renewal project.

Riding high, dry and safe on her new hull, the *Majestic* was permanently moored at the Public Landing near Riverfront Stadium, at the Foot of Broadway. The *Atta Boy* was still moored at the showboat's stern, her diesel engine and paddle wheel were removed making her non functional as a towboat. She served primarily as living quarters, dressing rooms, and storage.

The UC Players opened the season with *"The Drunkard,"* followed with *"Ten Nights in a Barroom, Once Upon A Mattress, How to Succeed in Business, The Boys From Syracuse, Antole, Funny Girl, Good News, George M., Musical Melodrama,"* and closed the last of October.

March 3, 1972, for the second time in her history, the *Atta Boy* was gutted by fire. They thought it was caused by a coal stove explosion. City firemen and crew from the towboat *Clare Beatty* rushed to the scene and brought the fire under control. The *Atta Boy* was rebuilt from the hull up, with a smaller superstructure, and used as the headboat in the city's new transient boat harbor.

The *Majestic* celebrated her golden anniversary in a special ceremony June 12, 1973. It also marked her sixth year of operation by the University of Cincinnati. Tommy and Ester were there for the ceremony. One speaker told the crowd, "Our aim is to continue the tradition set down by Captain Reynolds of bringing people together through fun and laughter. If we succeed, you'll keep coming back and that's what the Captain intended in 1923 and that's how it will always be," he promised.

Mayor Theodore Berry proclaimed June 12, 1973, as *Showboat Majestic Day.* A"Showboat Follies," was the main feature of the day. It included 50 songs representing each of the year of the *Majestic,* a melodrama *"No. No. A Million Times No,"* vaudeville acts, plus memorable scenes from the UC musicals. The show ran two evenings a week June through August 15th.

The *Majestic* was swept loose from her mooring January 20, 1978, and was carried downriver in the ice run. She hit the nearby bridge pier and kept going. After ramming into the willows she was brought to a safe landing on the opposite side of the river at Ludlow, Ky., three miles below Cincinnati.

The original *Goldenrod* Showboat was gutted by fire at St. Louis on June 2, 1962, and was rebuilt. It made the *Majestic* the sole survivor of the original showboats still operating in America. January 18, 1980 the *Majestic* was entered in the National Register of Historic Places. A bronze plaque on the head of the showboat commemorates the event. In 1989 the *Majestic* was designated a National Historic Landmark. "The Vessel Possesses National Significance In Commemorating The History Of The United States Of America," says another plaque.

Due to the loss and restoration of her double-decked cabin, the *Atta Boy* wasn't included in the nomination. She is still a part of her history and is permanently moored at the stern of the *Majestic.*

After Dad's death, Harry and I sold our home in Bellemeade and moved to Marion, Ohio to be near our daughter, Margaret Catherine, her husband, Ellis, and two children, Diana and Linda. I hadn't seen the boats since 1960 and with one look at the old homeplace, the tears began to roll. All the memories came rushing back. Except for the steel hull and red paint trim on the showboat, she looked the same, only Dad wasn't there.

Going on board, we had a pleasant visit with Rick Diehl who showed us around and talked showboating. That evening the river looked like an oil painting. The *Majestic's* lights twinkled and recorded calliope music welcomed the crowd gathering on board. It was like old times sitting there watching the theatre fill with happy chattering people.

The curtain rose on the show *"Egad, What A Cad."* The stage wasn't large enough to hold all the actors and a full orchestra at the same time. An upright piano on the left side of the stage and percussion were used. Scott Wolly, the Music Director and pianist, was in his fifth year with the *Majestic*. His rendition of Scott Joplin's ragtime hit, "The Entertainer," was spectacular.

I was glad we went and knew the *Majestic* was in good hands. As Rick Diehl told me, "We haven't tried to change the *Majestic* or make her all things to all people. Only soft drinks and hot pretzels are served along with our special kind of entertainment."

Their 1983 season opened with an announcement from Mayor Thomas B. Brush proclaiming April 10 through the 16th, as Showboat *Majestic* Week in honor of her 60th anniversary.

The UC Players continued to enjoy popularity on through their 1988 season, during which the *Majestic* celebrated her 66th birthday and her 21st year of service to Cincinnati. They presented *"Summer Rhapsody, It's Only a Play,"* and the *"Queen City Toast,"* and closed the season September 18th.

This was the final performance presented on the *Majestic* by the University of Cincinnati's Conservatory of Music. After producing and directing shows aboard the showboat for 21 years, Paul Rutledge was retiring and didn't renew his contract with the city.

Downie Productions, a Cincinnati based company, was selected to produce the shows on the *Majestic*. The project was supported by a grant from the Fine Arts Fund.

Downie Productions, with Jay Downie, Producer, presented the musicals *"Oklahoma, Cole, Cotton Patch Gospel,"* and *"George M,"* during the summer season. *"Dames at Sea, The Dining Room,"* and *"Gifts From The Heart,"* were presented their fall and winter season. They closed December 23, 1989.

Their 1990 season of musicals included *"Cotton Patch Gospel, You're A Good Man, Charlie Brown, Showboat Follies, The Sound of Music, I Do! I Do!,"* and *"My Fair Lady."*

Beginning with *"Cotton Patch Gospel,"* the showboat patrons were offered a dinner and show package with B&B Riverboats. At 5:30 patrons boarded the *B&B Riverboat* and enjoyed a scenic cruise up the Ohio River, ate dinner, and returned to the *Majestic* for the 8 o'clock performance.

Harry and I were invited to attend their premier performance of *"Cotton Patch Gospel."* We enjoyed it immensely.

We also attended *"Showboat Follies,"* June 7th. It took us down memory lane with beautiful Broadway songs, river medleys, dancing, and comedy bits reminiscent of our early vaudeville tours. A medley of patriotic songs brought everyone to their feet. The cast waved flags and the audience joined in singing the finale, "God Bless America."

I really felt at home this time aboard the boat. The atmosphere was right. Harry and I stood on the wharf watching Denny Thomas and his helper, John Warner, readying the *Majestic* for the evening performance. We lingered on deck looking at the beautiful Ohio with boats passing by, and listening to the nostalgic sound of the calliope record playing familiar songs in the background.

After the show a champagne reception was hosted by Jay Downie and everyone met the cast and staff members. Standing there on the front of the showboat gazing at the Cincinnati skyline, I thought, wouldn't Dad be proud that after all these years the *Majestic*, with her unforgettable "Cargo of Memories," lives on.

Cargo of Memories

Chapter 25
Calliope and Showboat Update

The Majestic's calliope remained in storage at Indiana University until the mid-sixties. At that time the Alumni Association placed the calliope in an ornately decorated circus wagon as part of their Bicentennial project. The wagon weighs six tons and has a 360 gallon water tank, boiler similar to ours, and a self contained generator to pump water and energize the now electronic calliope keyboard. On full thirty-pound steam the calliope can be heard for three miles.

Larry McPherson, who reconditioned the calliope and keeps it in perfect condition, is the calliopist. Its music can be heard all over the state playing for festivals and celebrations. Hooks Drug Store and the Kroger Company have been staunch supporters of the project.

I have played the calliope on several occasions at Celina, Ohio during their Lake Festival and in the park at Greenville, Ohio during their 175th Treaty Festival.

The *Majestic's* calliope was the last authentic showboat calliope heard along the Ohio River, its tributaries, and the Mississippi River. Thanks to the Indiana University Alumni Association, the *Majestic's* calliope and its music are being preserved for posterity.

The *Majestic* showboat's 1991 season at Cincinnati is administered by the Cincinnati Recreation Commission, with Tom Perrino, Showboat Coordinator. In addition to concerts and special presentations, plays and musicals were presented by The Cincinnati Young People's Theatre, Beechmount Players, and the Northern Kentucky University Theatre Department.

Plays and musicals presented were, *"Dr. Browndog's Monkeytime, My Name is Alice, Stepping Out, Blue Plate Special, Plaza Suite, Earnest In Love, Stardust,"* and *"1976."*

"The End"

Cargo of Memories

Copyright Acknowledgments

Cargo of Memories

12 –· The Showboat News, August 24, 1929, page 72. © 19 by
Billboard Publications, Inc.

Chapter 9
13 – Letter written by Captain Reynolds from November 9, 1929,
page 74. © 19 by Billboard Publications, Inc.

14 – America Ends Good Season – William Reynolds Beats P.A.
on Candy Sales Charge, October 5, 1929, page 74. © BPI
Communications, Inc. Used with permission from Billboard.

Chapter 12
15 – Majestic Showboat on its way downriver, August 11, 1934,
page 134. © BPI Communications, Inc. Used with permission
from Billboard

16 – Letter from DeWitt Kirk, August 25, 1934, page 135. © 1934,
BPI Communications, Inc. Used with permission from
Billboard.

17 – Closing Notice of the Show, October 27, 1934, page 135.
© BPI Communications, Inc. Used with permission from
Billboard.

18 – Postcard from Hap Moore, July 15, 1936, page 139. © 1934,
1936 (respectively) BPI Communications, Inc. Used with
permission from Billboard.

Chapter 13
19 – Showboat Opened Engagement Here, May 14, 1937, page
144. The Parkersburg News.

20 – Majestic Pleases Audience, May 16, 1937, page 145. The
Parkersburg News.

21 – Over the Waves With Miss Fisher – On the Showboat, June
1937, page 145. East Liverpool News.

Chapter 16
22 – Showboat Coming Thrusday, May 8, 1941, page 165.
Parkersburg, W. Va. News.

23 – Good Crowds at Showboat Here, May 15, 1941, page 165.
Parkersburg News.

37 – Showboat Moves On, June 28, 1956, page 194. The Wellsville Ohio Press.

38 – The Majestic Coming Back Again, June 11, 1958, page 195. The Point Pleasant Register.

39 – Showboat Majestic Makes River Rock, August 5, 1958, page 196. The Pittsburg Press.

Chapter 22
40 – Dad's reply to a reporter about quitting the showboat business, page 200. The Point Pleasant Register.

Chapter 23
41 – It was a sad day for Mason County river boat fans, May 5, 1960, page 202. "Where the Water Mingles," by the late Mary Hyre, The Athens Messenger and Point Pleasant Register.

42 – Last Showboat on the Ohio Preserves an Era, June 8, 1960, page 204. The Point Pleasant Register.

Index